THEN & NOW®

SAN PEDRO

OPPOSITE: Mary Star of the Sea, originally located on the corner of West Ninth and Centre Streets, has served the spiritual needs of San Pedro's Catholic community since 1889. This wooden church, dedicated January 1, 1905, was the second building on this Vinegar Hill district site. Services were conducted here until the church relocated to the 800 block of West Eighth Street in the late 1950s. Townhouses now occupy that property, but a house that was behind this church in the 1900s is still in use today. That house is slightly visible on the far right of the present-day photograph. (Courtesy of San Pedro Bay Historical Society.)

THEN & NOW®

SAN PEDRO

Jim Isaac and Tom Herrera

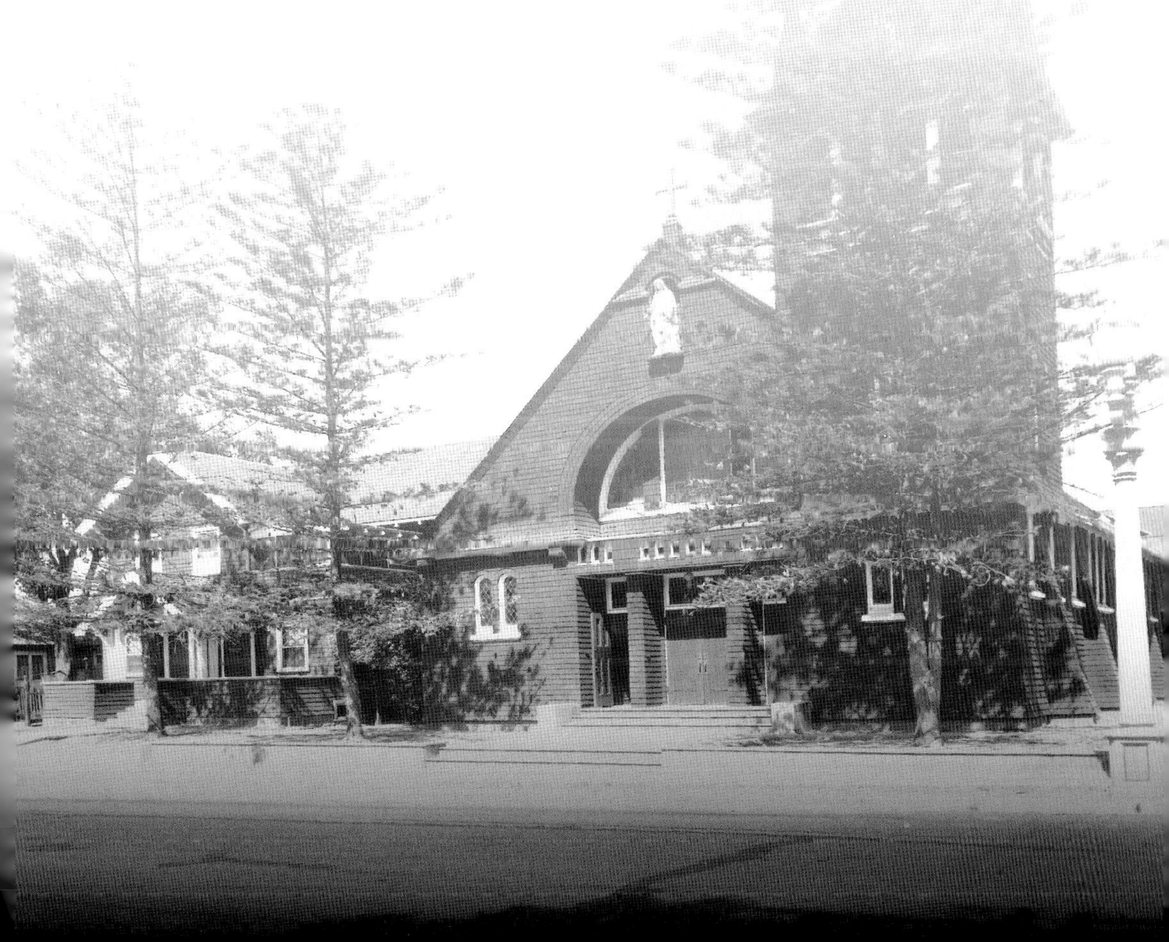

We dedicate this book to Hailey Nicole Herrera, first born of Amber and Michael Herrera. Hopefully Hailey will enjoy the book when she is old enough to read it.

ISBN 978-0-7385-8199-6

Library of Congress Control Number: 2010934816

Published by Arcadia Publishing
Charleston, South Carolina

Printed in the United States of America

For all general information, please contact Arcadia Publishing:
Telephone 843-853-2070
Fax 843-853-0044
E-mail sales@arcadiapublishing.com
For customer service and orders:
Toll-Free 1-888-313-2665

Visit us on the Internet at www.arcadiapublishing.com

On the Front Cover: This present-day view of Beacon Street at Sixth Street looks south. The building on the left once held offices for American President Lines. The Sunrise Hotel on the right takes up the eastern half of the city block. The *then* image depicts Beacon Street, looking south at Sixth Street. Nob Hill can be seen in the far background of this photograph taken around 1910. The building with the clock tower is the Bank of San Pedro. Across the street from the bank is the western side of the Alexander Hotel. (Courtesy of San Pedro Bay Historical Society.)

On the Back Cover: This photograph, taken around 1910, was shot at Seventh and Beacon Streets, looking north. On the right is the newly constructed city hall, which was completed in 1909, and the Ferl building is on the left. The San Pedro Emergency Hospital was located in the Ferl building at this time. San Pedro's municipal building, which was completed in 1928, is now on the city hall property, and the Ferl building is now a parking lot. (Courtesy of San Pedro Bay Historical Society.)

Contents

Acknowledgments

Acknowledgments of those who helped with the writing of this book must start with a vigorous thank you to Joe McKinzie, president of the San Pedro Bay Historical Society. His Arcadia book, *Postcard History Series: San Pedro*, was the genesis for this project. *San Pedro Then & Now* was originally only meant to be a multimedia presentation based on Joe's book for a fourth-grade class, but somehow it took on a life of its own and became a book.

The San Pedro Bay Historical Society made this book possible. With the expert assistance of the head archivist, Anne Hansford, the society's extensive collection of vintage photographs, newspaper clippings, and publications—such as Kathryn Schultz's *San Pedro Public Schools*—were invaluable resources. Al Bitonio was particularly helpful when it came to navigating through old maps and pinpointing locations where photographs were taken. Thank you to them and other society volunteers.

The outstanding cooperation of Seaside Pharmacy management is gratefully recognized for supplying vintage photographs and information. The staff of Los Angeles councilwoman Janice Hahn's San Pedro field office deserves thanks for making it possible to take the *now* photograph of the municipal ferry building that appears in this book. A volunteer at the Los Angeles City Fire Department San Pedro Museum located in old Fire Station 36 at the municipal building was helpful in tracking down the location of old Fire Boat House No. 1.

Stephanie Williams deserves our recognition for assisting and putting up with us on some of our photograph shoots. It wasn't easy.

The Port of Los Angeles was kind in supplying us with a brief history of San Pedro and the Port of Los Angeles.

For guiding us through the maze of writing and putting together this book, our hats are off to Jerry Roberts, our editor.

Finally Brenda Herrera—Tom's mother—gets a thank you. It was her firmly asking us, "Why don't you guys write a book?" one day two years ago that probably motivated us into seriously thinking about this project.

To all those mentioned, thanks a million!

Unless otherwise credited, *then* photographs were used courtesy of San Pedro Bay Historical Society. All *now* photographs were taken by Tom Herrera and Jim Isaac.

INTRODUCTION

San Pedro, California, is a community rich in history and culture. The city of San Pedro was incorporated into the city of Los Angeles on August 28, 1909. Thanks in part to the opening of the Panama Canal in 1914, the Port of Los Angeles and San Pedro became a strategic stop for international trade, leading to the creation of various industries and growth and development. There were many events and key political figures that led to San Pedro becoming a prominent port city.

According to the Port of Los Angeles, on October 8, 1542, a Portuguese explorer by the name of Juan Rodriguez Cabrillo came across a marshland and natural harbor at the northwest end of San Pedro Bay. He named the area Bahia de Los Fumas, or "Bay of Smokes," after the smoke that rose from the nearby hillside inhabited by Native American hunters.

In 1769, Spanish officials and missionaries set their sights on colonizing the West Coast, which ultimately led to the first commercial ventures in San Pedro in the mid-1800s. By the time California joined the United States in 1848, business in San Pedro harbor was flourishing. A host of politicians, businessmen, and community visionaries are responsible for San Pedro Bay fulfilling its ultimate destiny of becoming the largest cargo gateway into North America. One such visionary was Phineas Banning, who founded Wilmington and was nicknamed the "Father of Los Angeles Harbor."

Banning's entrepreneurialism and influence positioned the port for future success as the maritime and trade center for a rapidly growing West Coast city. Another person to play an important role in the development of San Pedro Bay was Stephen M. White, also called the "Savior of the Bay." White, a senator from California, stood up to big business and political forces, pushing through regulations that led Congress to declare San Pedro Bay the official port for Los Angeles in 1897.

The city of Los Angeles and the harbor area experienced unparalleled population growth in the early 20th century. The cities of San Pedro and Wilmington were incorporated into the city of Los Angeles on August 28, 1909, making the Port of Los Angeles an official department of the city of Los Angeles.

By 1912, dredging and widening of the main channel and the completion of major sections of the federal breakwater enabled the port to accommodate larger vessels. When the Panama Canal opened in 1914, it gave the Port of Los Angeles a unique strategic position for international trade. Various industries began popping up in and around the port. Fishing, canneries, oil drilling, and shipbuilding were major industries that generated jobs and commerce in Los Angeles and, especially, San Pedro.

Over the years, the face of San Pedro, as well as the topography, has changed dramatically. Some changes included the lowering or cutting of street elevations, which leveled buildings and/or forced the move of buildings many blocks. The 1933 Long Beach earthquake caused severe damage to many of the brick buildings, forcing demolition or major reconstruction and remodeling. The Beacon Street Redevelopment Project in the early 1970s was a major renovation.

Imagine having the ability to stand at a location and turn back the clock, viewing past moments in time and answering questions about the fascinating history of what life looked like then and what once stood there. The purpose of this book is to be that time machine: to take the reader on that extraordinary expedition and compare present-day photographs with historical images taken during the growth of the city and port.

With images and information provided by the San Pedro Bay Historical Society, firsthand accounts from the residents of historical buildings, and a little Indiana Jones–style persistence, lets take a journey through the past and present—the then and now of San Pedro and the Port of Los Angeles.

CHAPTER 1

Schools, Churches, and Libraries

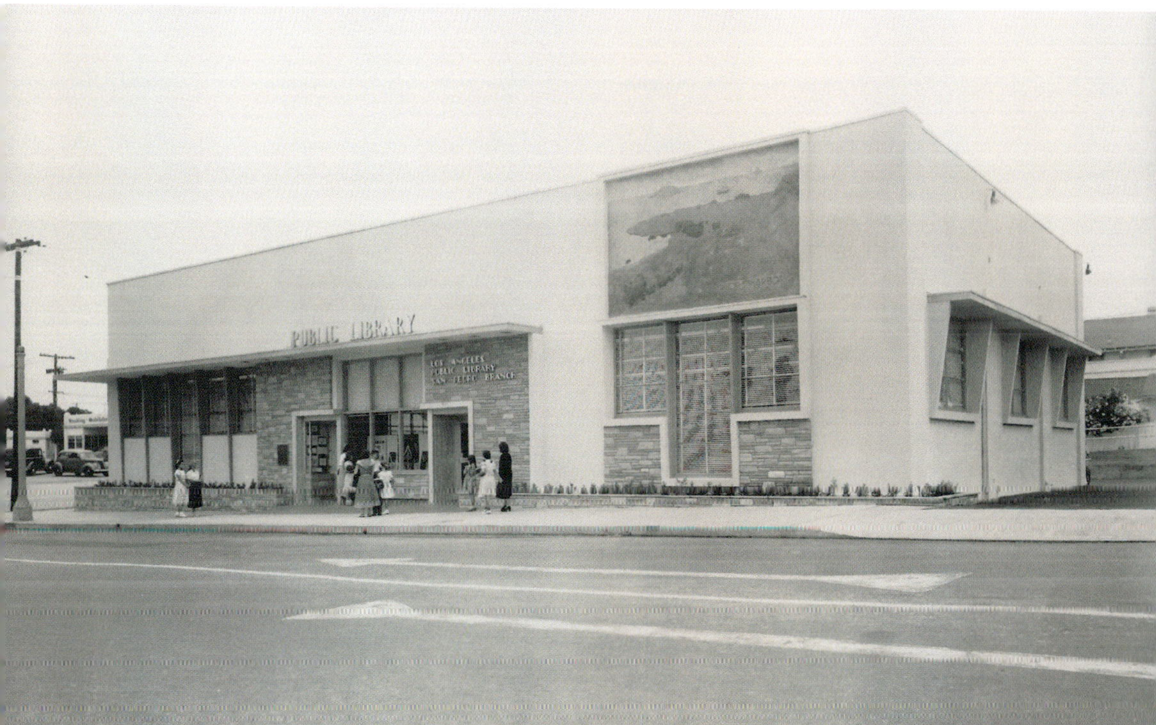

Educational, spiritual, and intellectual institutions are very important and major factors in the history of San Pedro. Some of the oldest schools, churches, and libraries in Southern California are located in the harbor community. Pictured is San Pedro's third library, completed in 1948 on the corner of Gaffey and Tenth Streets. It replaced the brick library building that stood on this lot since 1924 but was condemned as unsafe in 1943. The 1948 library has since been demolished and replaced with a modern, larger facility completed in 1983.

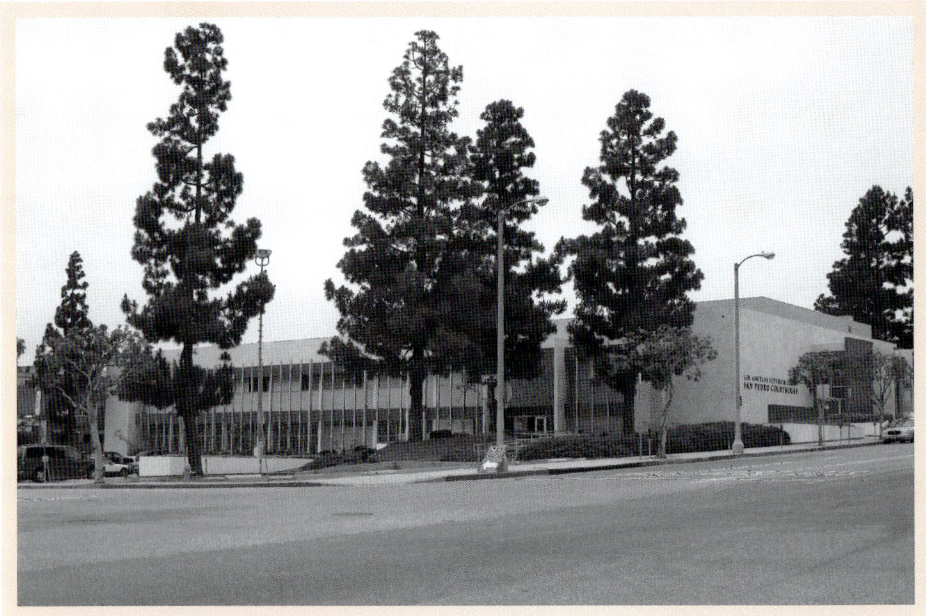

The photograph below shows the 1919 brick building that replaced a wooden schoolhouse that had been on that site since 1885. Fifth Street School was San Pedro's first public school located between Fifth and Sixth Streets on Centre Street. By the late 1920s, San Pedro's central business district surrounded the school. It was thought that the area was not the best environment for students. The school was demolished in 1927. The school built to replace it, Cabrillo Avenue School, opened that same year. A Los Angeles superior court building is presently located on that property.

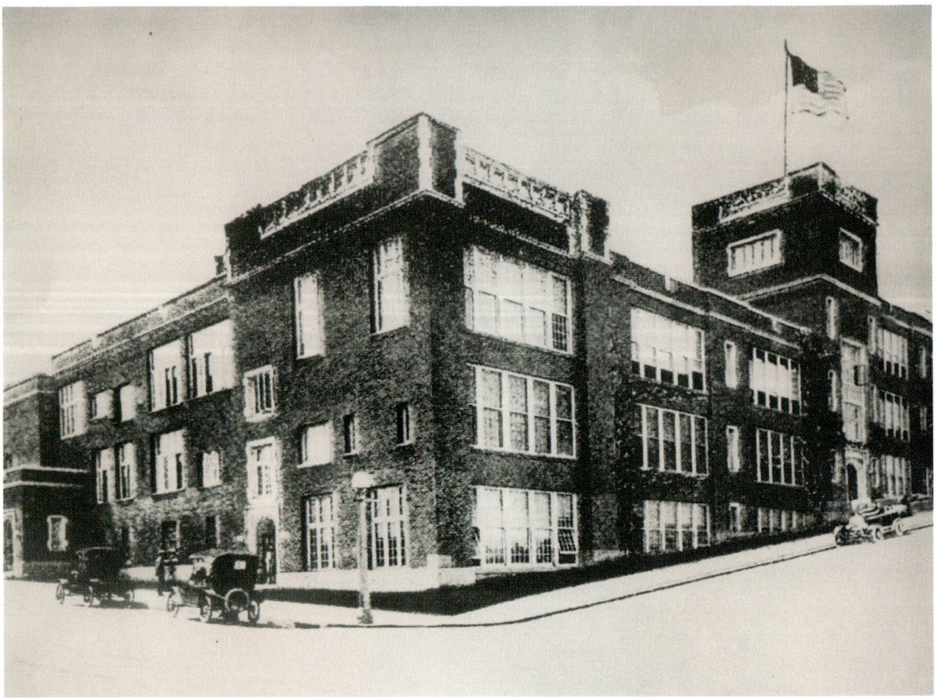

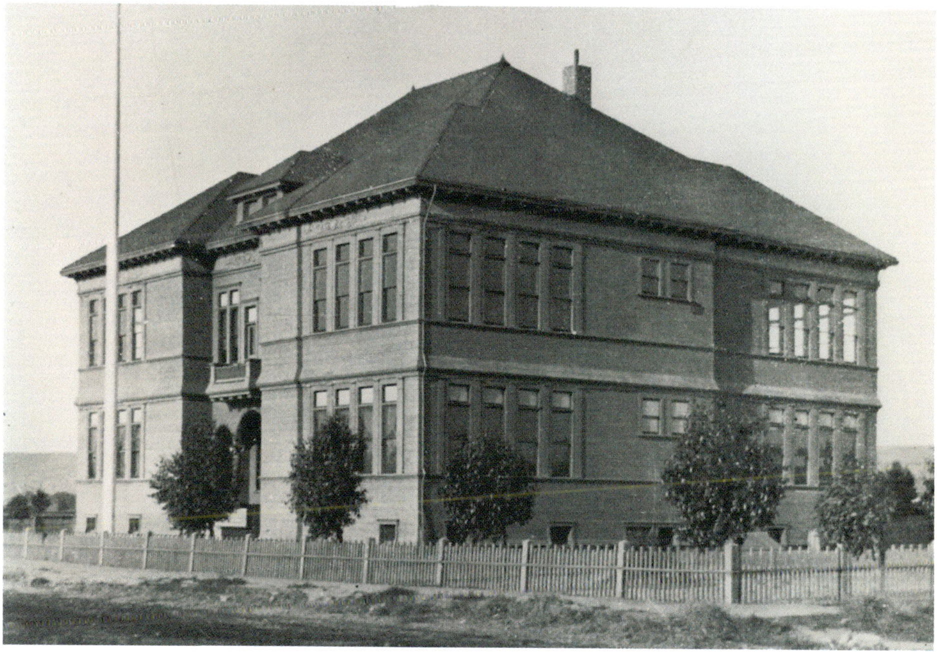

Sixteenth Street School has a unique place in the history of San Pedro schools. During the earlier years of the school's existence, it accommodated children in grades kindergarten to high school. High school classes were conducted on the upper floor of the building from 1903 to 1905. The original wooden structure of the Sixteenth Street School was totally destroyed by fire in June 1922. Classes were held in tents until a new permanent structure was available. Some of the main structures of the present-day school are what replaced the fire-damaged wooden building. The name of the school was changed from Sixteenth Street School to Fifteenth Street School for the simple reason that when San Pedro was incorporated into Los Angeles in 1909, the Los Angeles School District already had a Sixteenth Street School. Present-day Fifteenth Street School is on the school's original site, and since the demolition of the Fifth Street School, it is the oldest operating school in San Pedro.

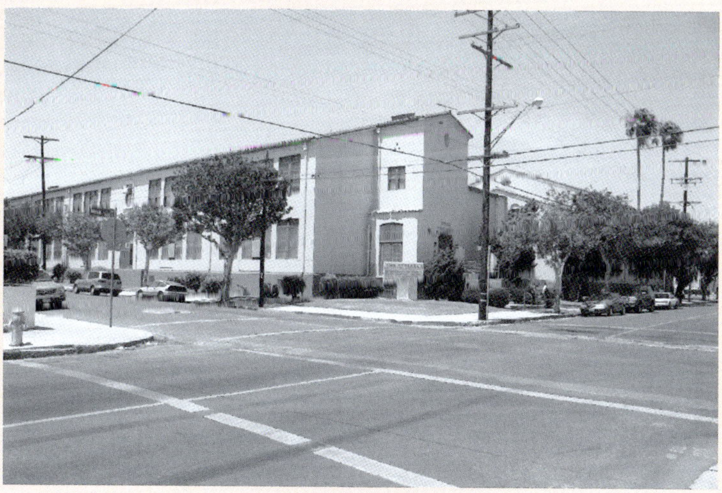

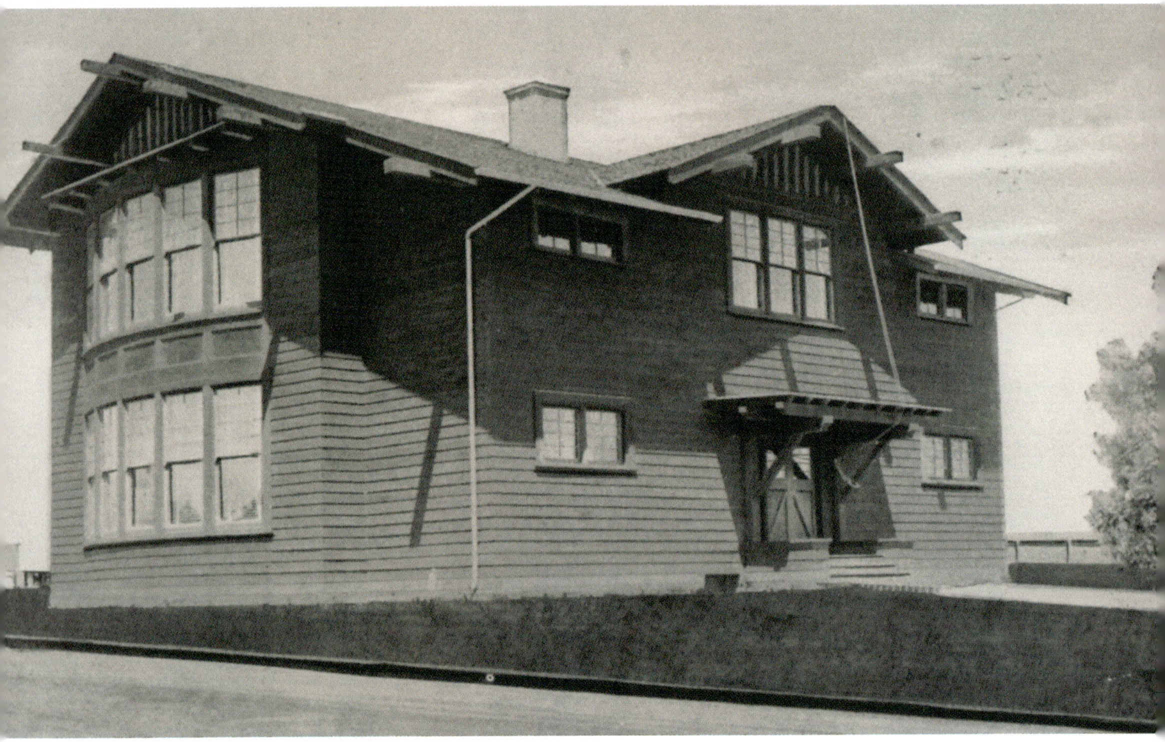

To meet the needs of San Pedro's growing population, a school was erected on land in an area known as Barton Hill (named after past San Pedro postmaster Alberta Barton). The school was built in 1905, as seen in the postcard above postmarked 1919. By 1917, it was decided a larger school was needed. That building stands on the site today. It was not damaged during the 1933 Long Beach earthquake, but as a precaution, children attended classes in tents and bungalows until certain structures on the building were removed. The building was reinforced and covered with stucco. Except for a few alterations, present-day Barton Hill School looks much the same as it did after the 1933 renovation.

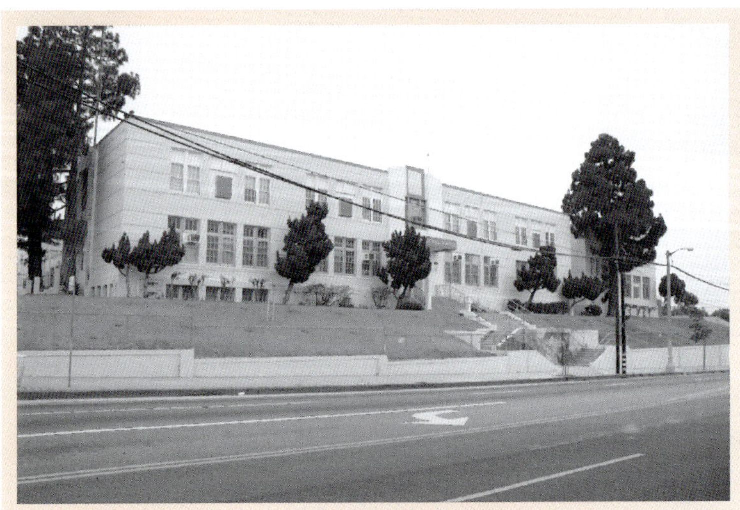

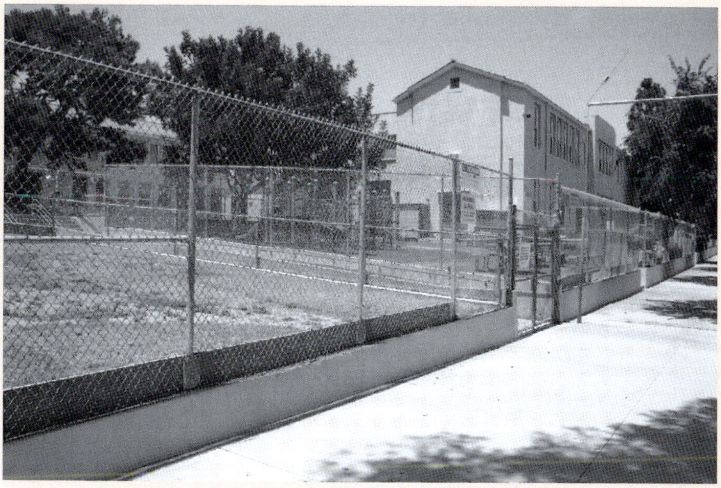

Point Fermin Elementary School was the first new school built since San Pedro was incorporated into Los Angeles in 1909. A portable bungalow was the school's first building when it opened in 1912. Growing enrollment and the necessity to teach more than three grades prompted the purchase of more land in 1919 for a larger, permanent building. The present-day, two-story brick building opened in 1922. This school was heavily damaged in the 1933 Long Beach earthquake. Students attended half-day sessions in tents until renovation was completed. The major structures of the school have not changed much in its 1933 renovation. Point Fermin school is the fourth oldest school in San Pedro, preceded by Fifth Street, Sixteenth/Fifteenth Street, and Barton Hill schools.

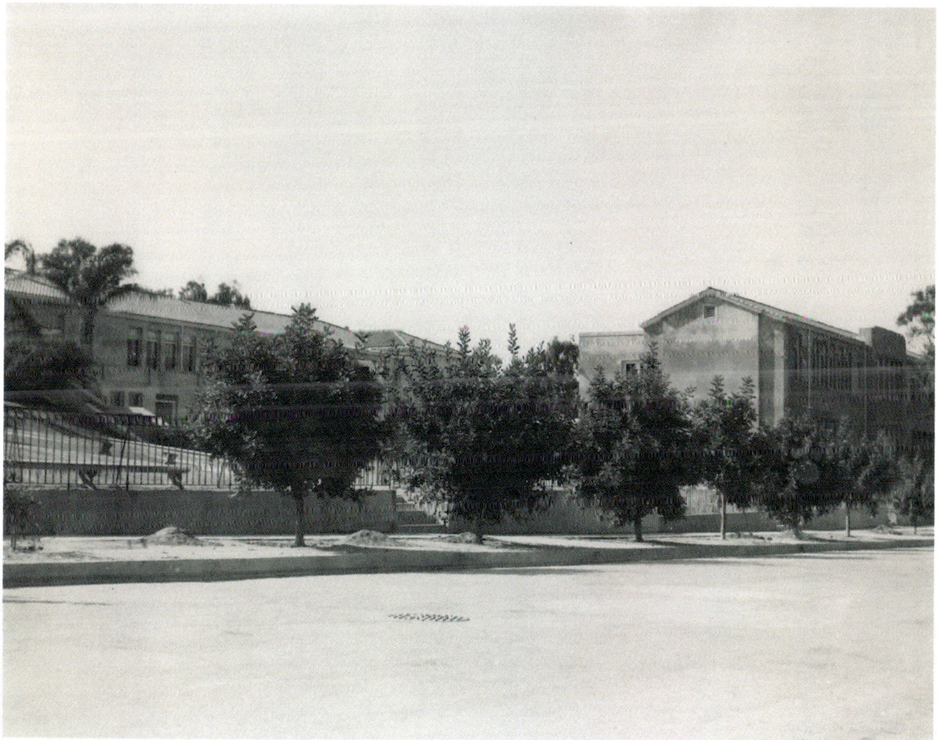

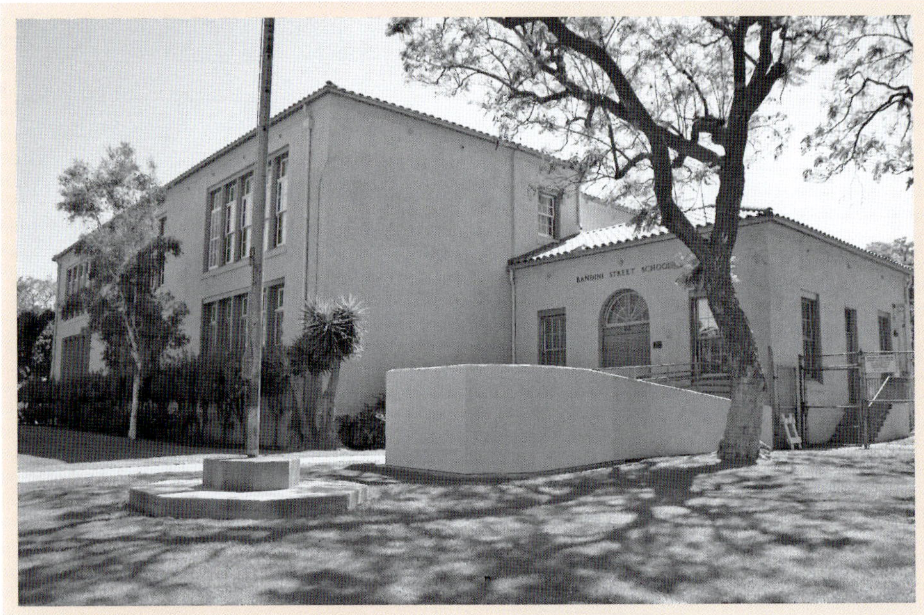

Named for the street it was built on, Bandini Street School opened in 1922 on land purchased from San Pedro real estate magnate George H. Peck. The school building has not changed much over the years. After the 1933 Long Beach earthquake, the brick walls were covered with stucco and damaged ornamentation was removed. Classes were held in tents until the school was repaired. The present-day photograph above shows that the building has changed very little since its renovation. Even the original flagpole foundation is still in use.

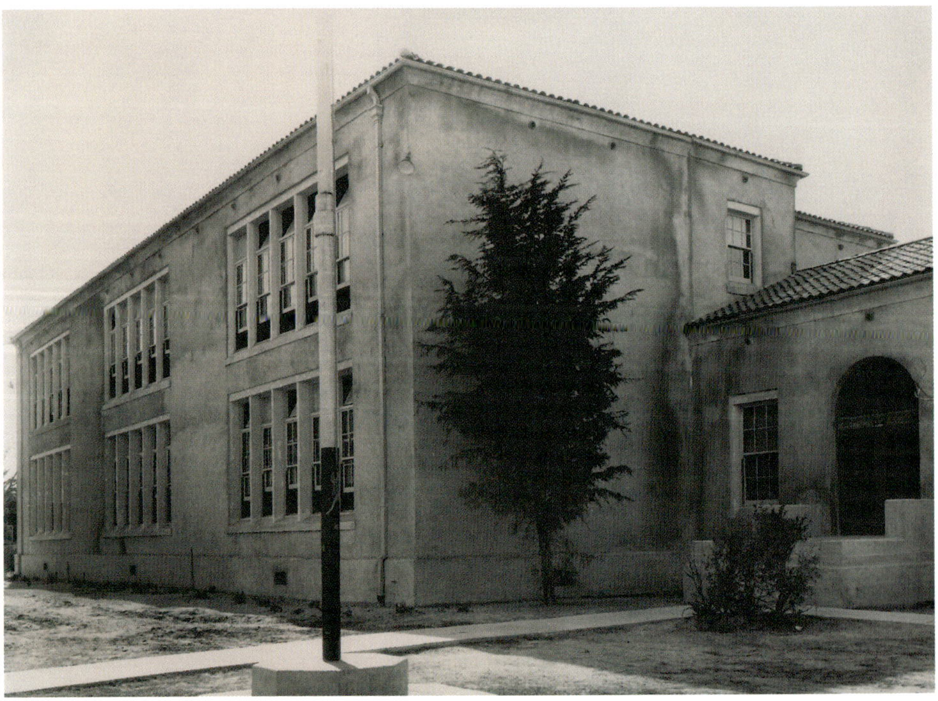

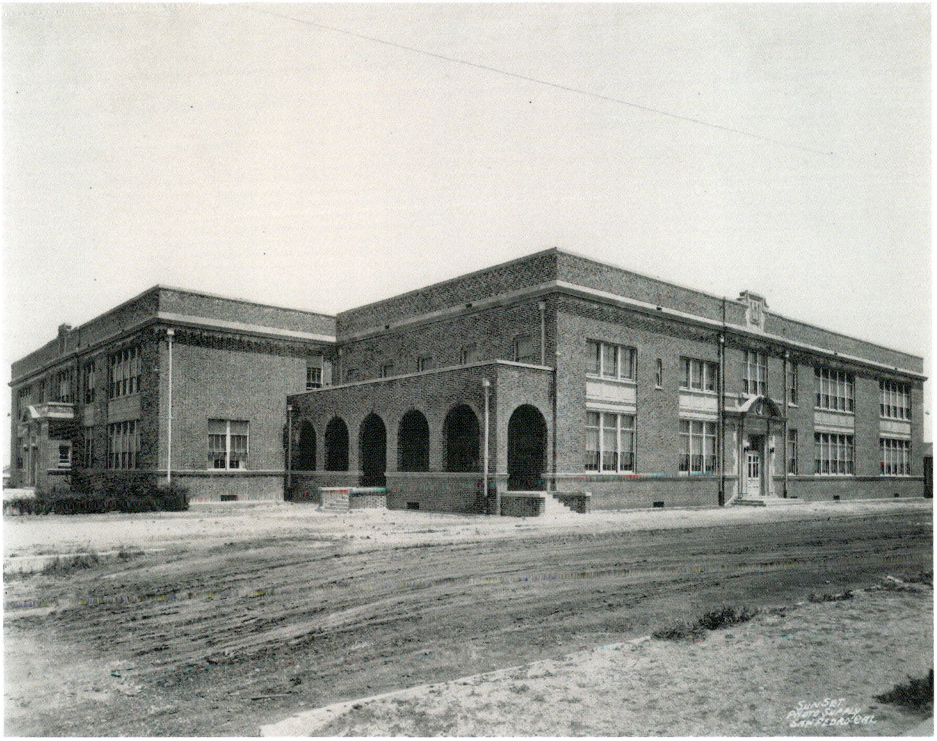

Leland Street Elementary School, pictured in the 1923 photograph above, is located at the 2100 block of South Leland Street. It opened as a result of a petition by residents in the area campaigning for a school. The original two-story brick building had 12 classrooms. The 1933 Long Beach earthquake damaged it to the point that architectural changes had to be made. Cement ornamentation on the exterior was removed, and the brick exterior was covered with stucco. A northern wing of the main building, shown in the 1923 photograph, was not rebuilt. Additional classrooms have been constructed on the school's property, and some alterations have been made to the main building. Present-day Leland Street Elementary School is very different from the original structure.

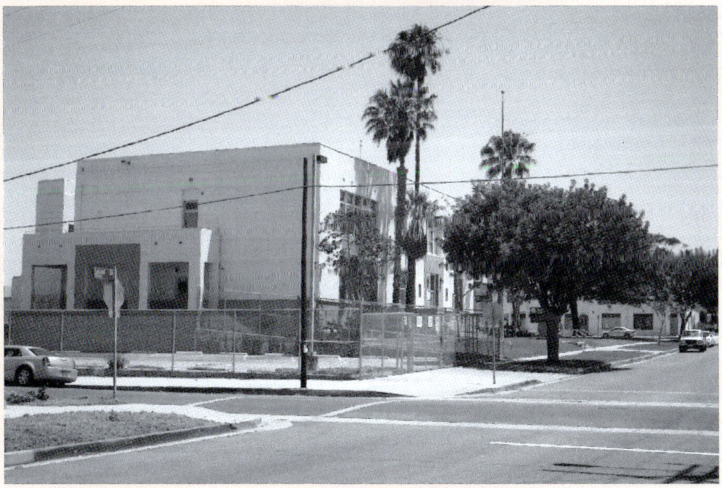

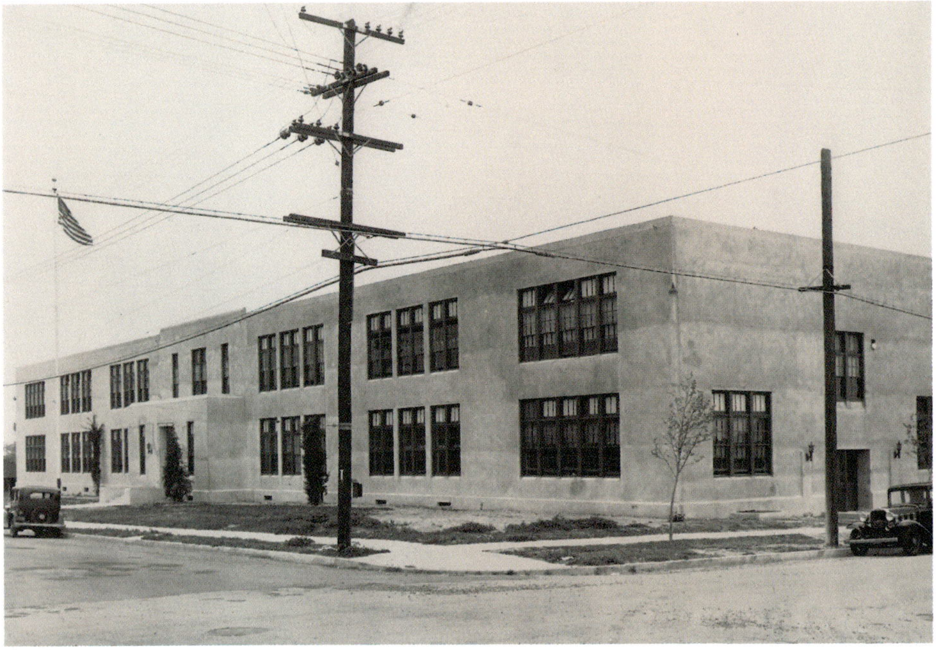

Cabrillo Avenue School, as seen in the *c.* 1927 photograph above, came into being as a result of San Pedro's population growing west of Pacific Avenue. It should also be noted that another factor was the discontent of San Pedro's growing central business area merchants with children loitering in the vicinity after Fifth Street School in the center of the city was dismissed. Or as it was more diplomatically put, it was not a good environment for children. Cabrillo Avenue School, located west of South Pacific Avenue, opened in 1927 to replace Fifth Street School. The school was not large enough to house the entire enrollment of Fifth Street School, so children were sent to other area schools. The 1933 Long Beach earthquake damaged the school enough for it to be declared unsafe. Tents were used as classrooms until the fall of 1935, when repairs to the school were completed. The main building of present-day Cabrillo Avenue School has not been altered much since.

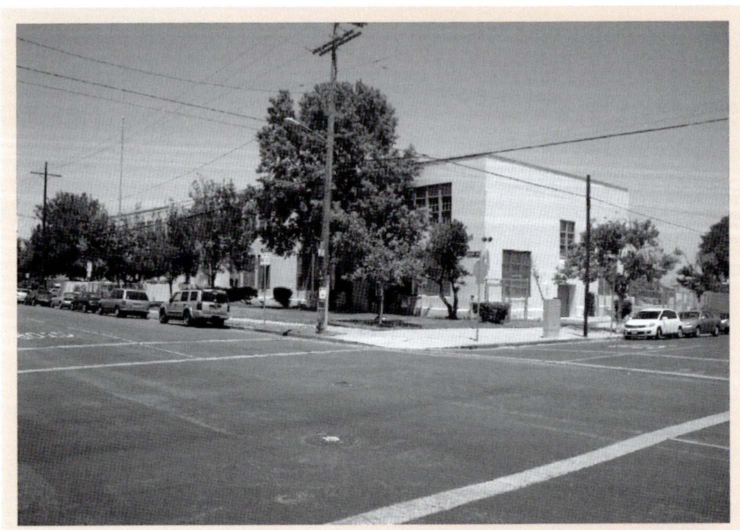

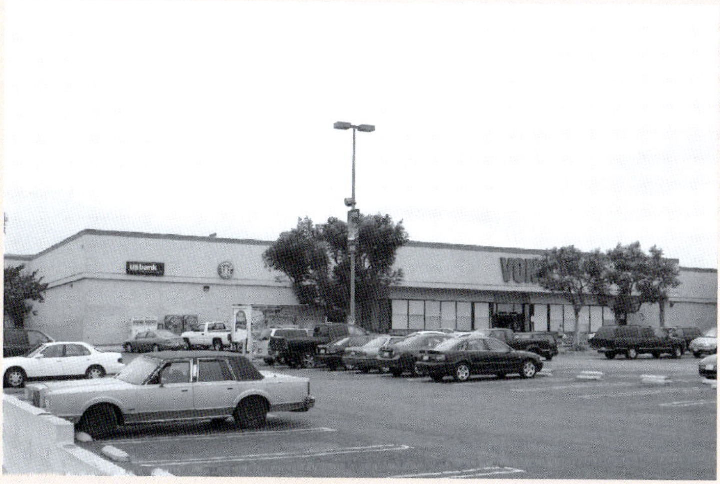

San Pedro High School did not have its own permanent building when it started in 1903. It was located on the upper floor of Sixteenth (now Fifteenth) Street School. Students began attending classes in the high school building located at 1221 South Gaffey Street in 1906. The 1933 Long Beach earthquake damaged this building, and a new school was built at its present-day location southwest of this site. Presently a Vons Market stands at that location and has the same address as the first San Pedro High School building.

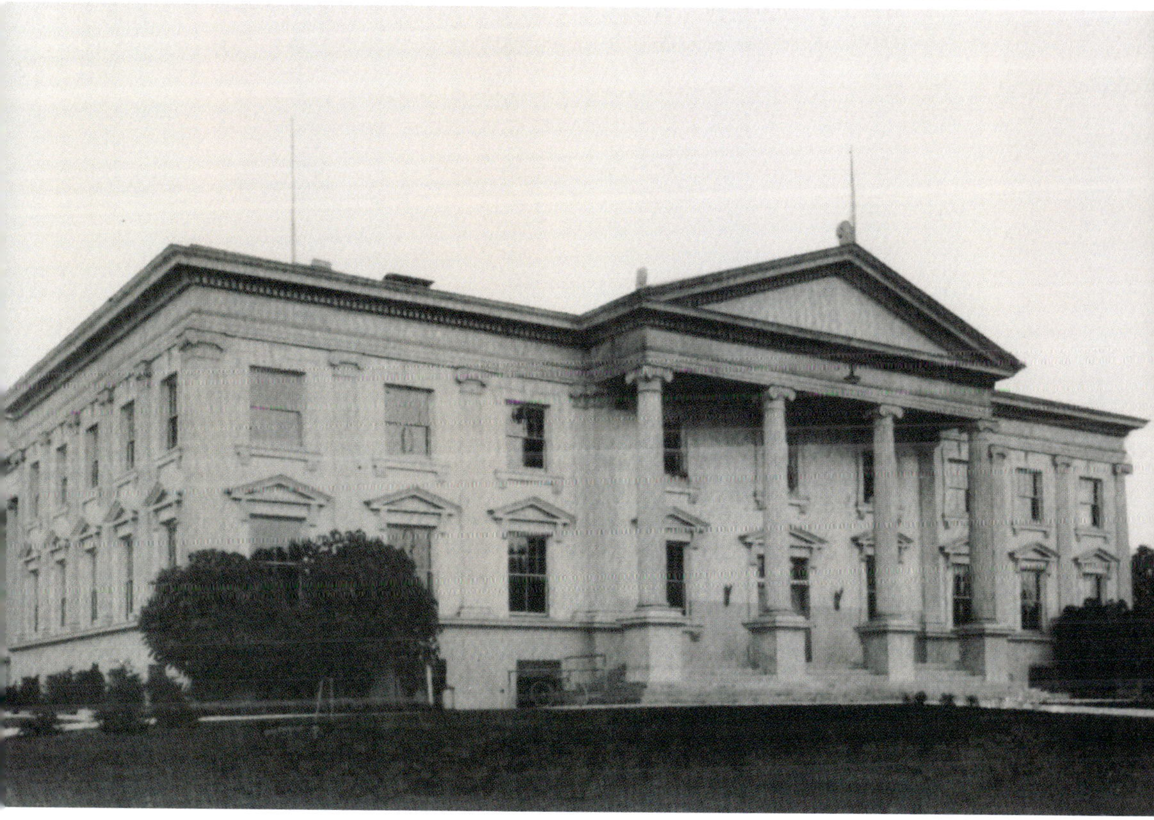

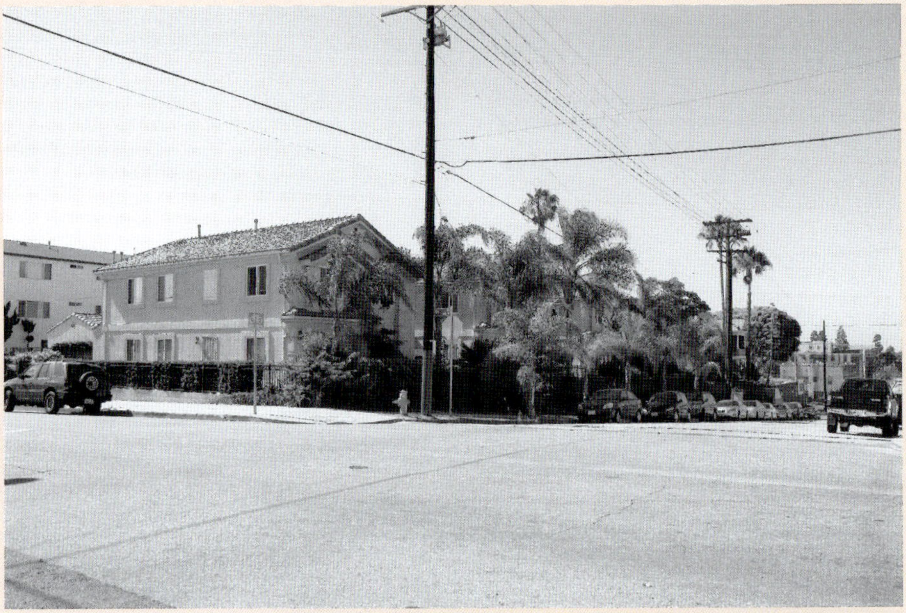

Mary Star of the Sea, originally located on the corner of West Ninth and Centre Streets, has served the spiritual needs of San Pedro's Catholic community since 1889. This wooden church, dedicated January 1, 1905, was the second building on this Vinegar Hill district site. Services were conducted here until the church relocated to the 800 block of West Eighth Street in the late 1950s. Townhouses now occupy that property, but a house that was behind this church in the 1900s is still in use today. That house is slightly visible on the far right of the present-day photograph.

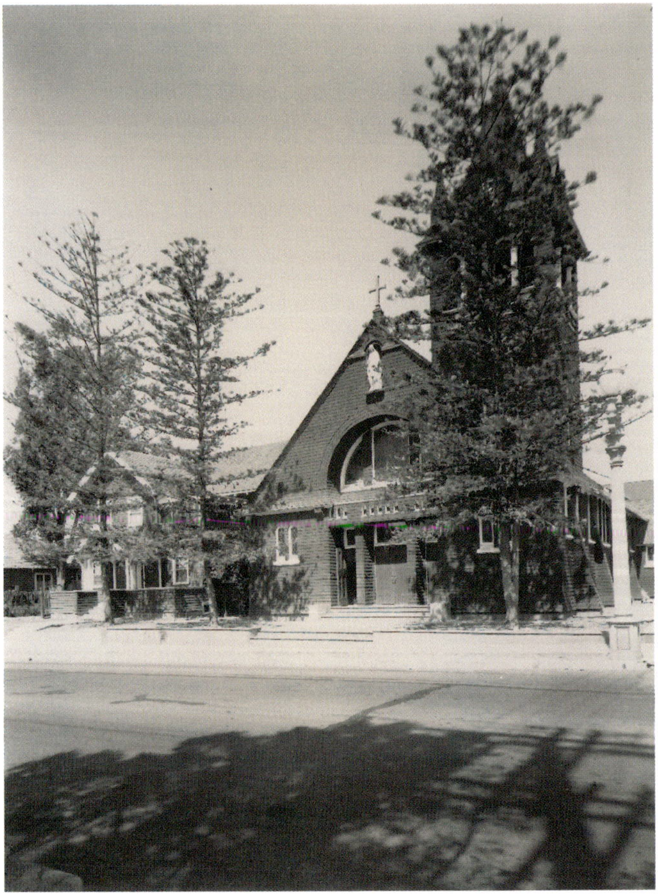

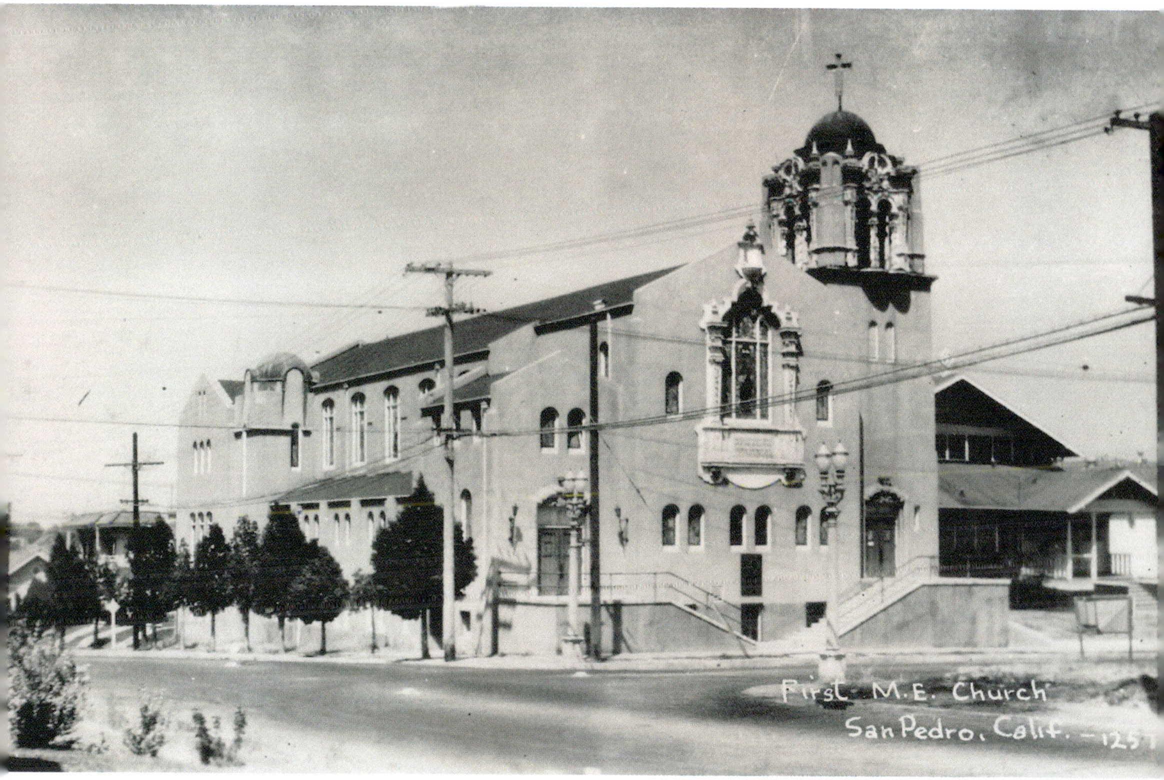

The grand building of the First Methodist Episcopal has been located on the northeast corner of Sixth and Grand Streets since 1923. This building has undergone more changes than any other building pictured in this book. By the time the 1931 photograph below was taken, the 1923 brick exterior had been covered with stucco.

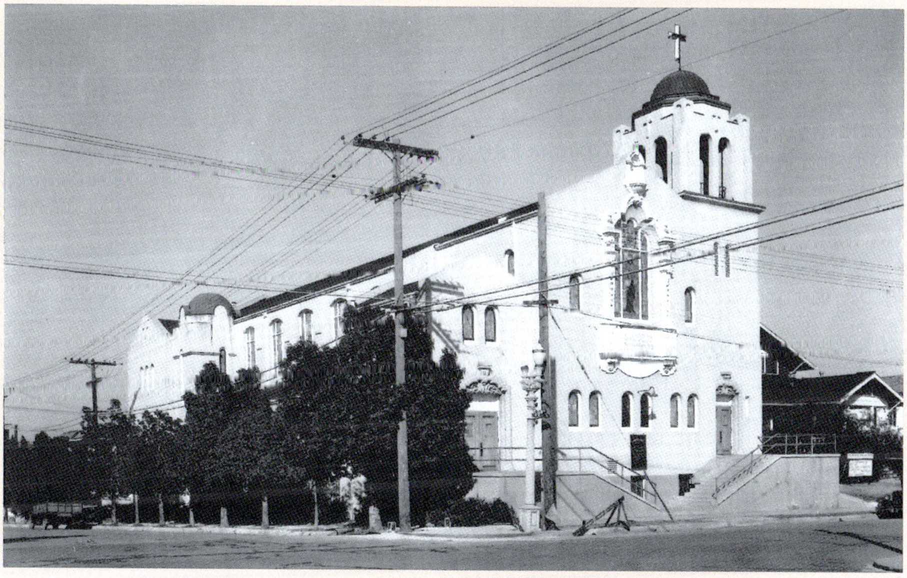

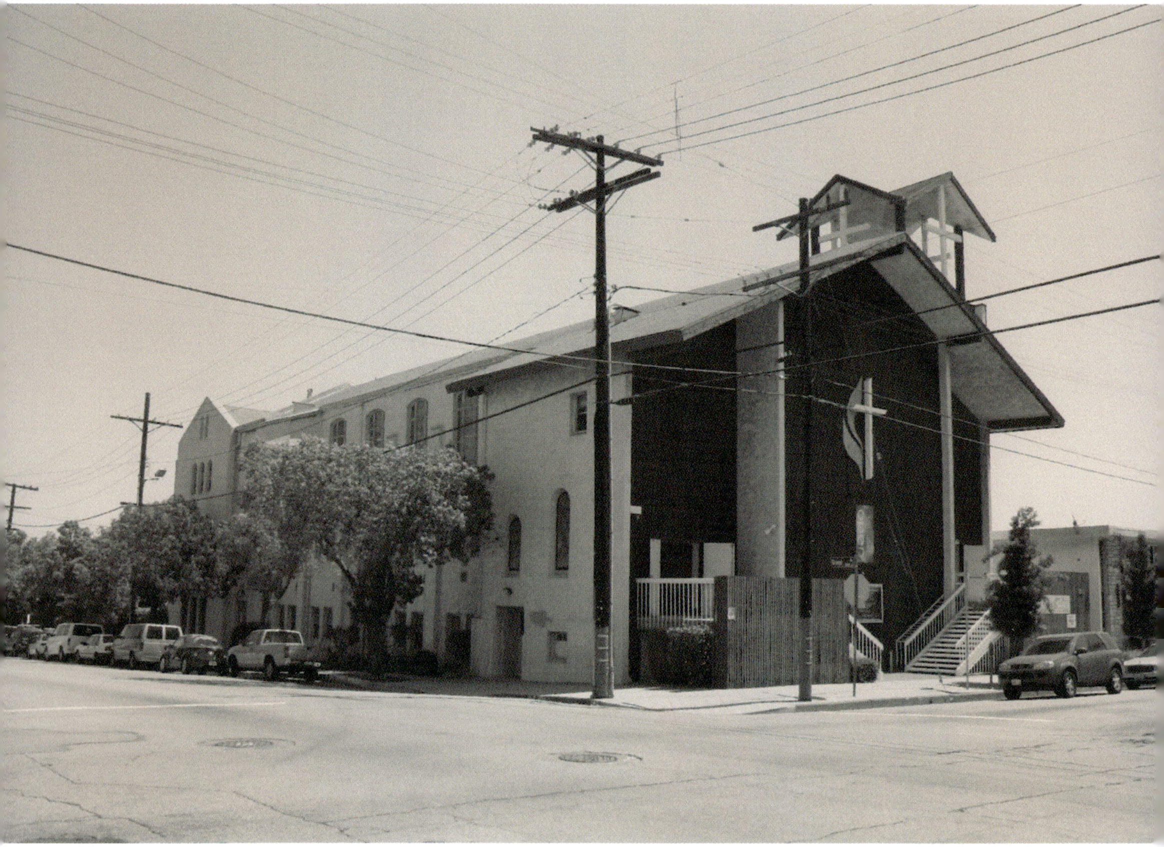

These contemporary photographs taken in 2008 and 2010 of the church—now the San Pedro United Methodist Church—show major modifications made to the church's exterior. The latest renovations, which again displayed the stained glass window, were completed in the summer of 2010.

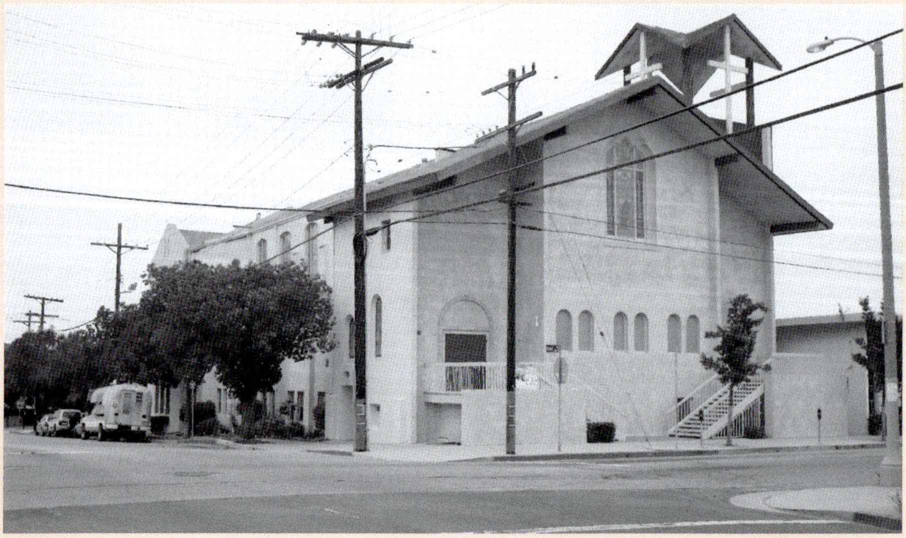

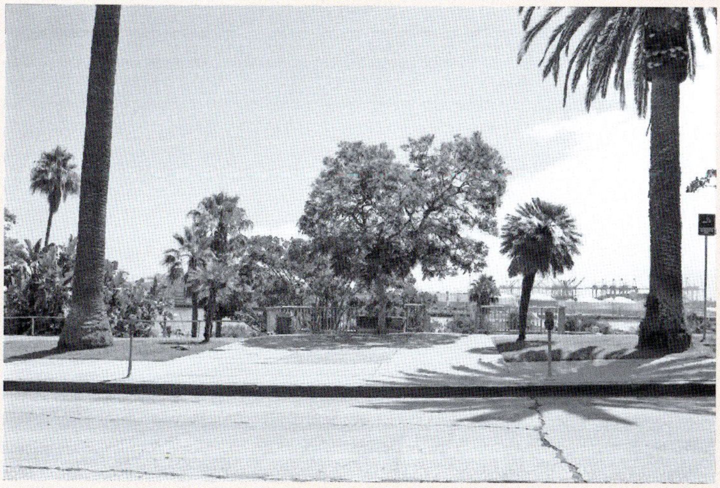

The subject of the photograph below is the September 9, 1935, ground-breaking ceremony for the new post office and U.S. Customs House. The domed building in the background was the Carnegie Library from 1906 to 1923. The initial grant to build the library was awarded by the Carnegie Corporation of New York. From 1924 until it was demolished in the mid-1960s, it was the San Pedro Chamber of Commerce. The Maritime Industry Memorial now occupies the library site, which is across the street from the post office that was completed in 1936.

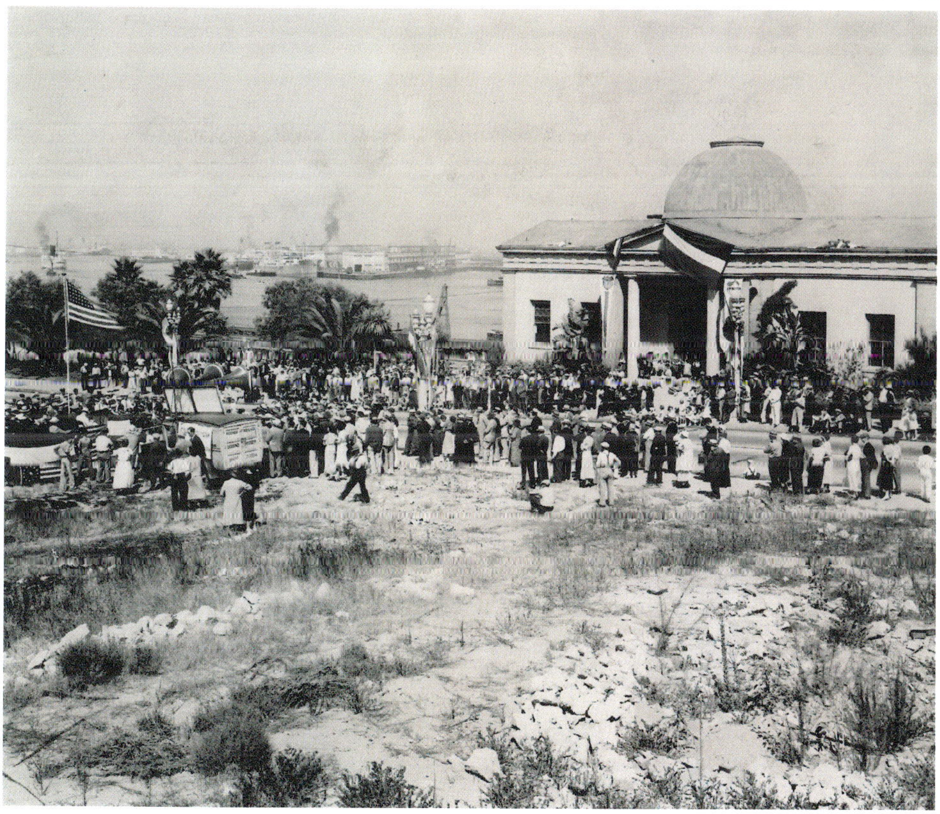

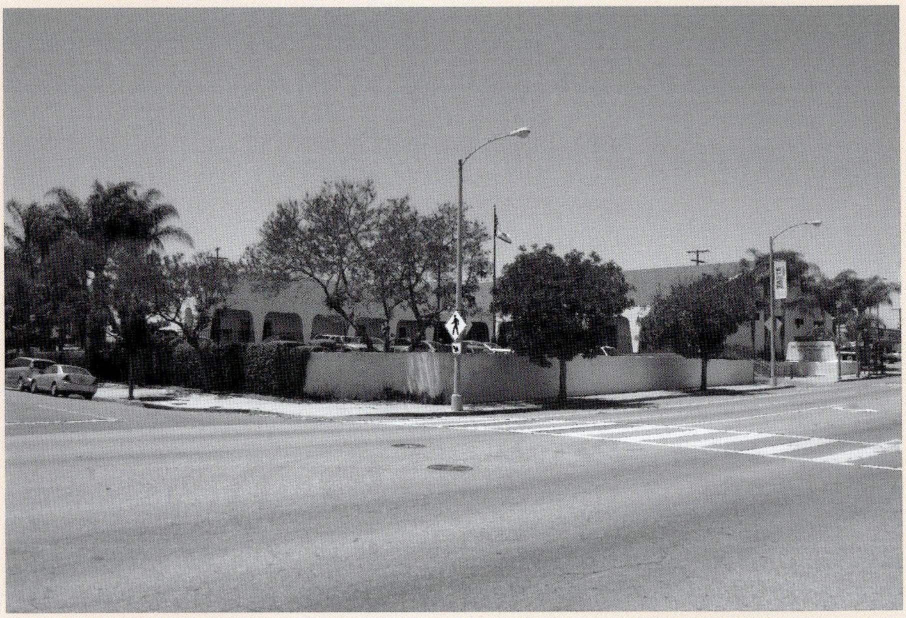

Because of changing industrial conditions in the area, as well as other factors, the Carnegie Library on Beacon Street could no longer provide efficient library services. In 1924, a new library was constructed on a lot at Tenth and Gaffey Streets to replace the Carnegie branch. In 1948, the building was replaced with a modern facility after being declared unsafe in 1943. The present-day library facility opened in 1983. The main building is on Ninth and Gaffey Streets. The site of previous libraries (brick fence in foreground) is now a parking lot for the present-day branch.

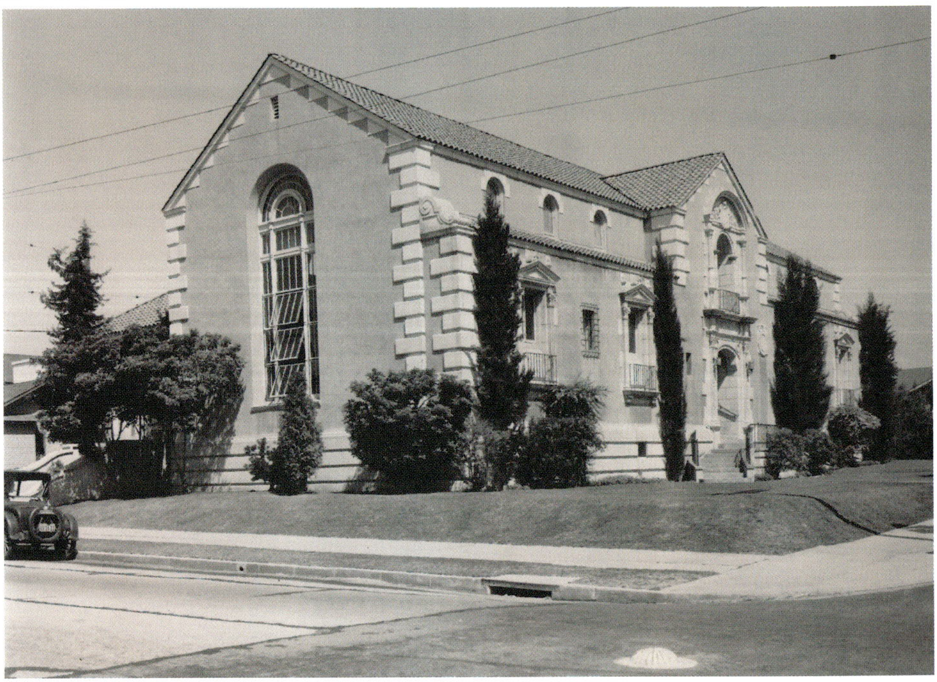

CHAPTER 2

THE STREETS OF SAN PEDRO

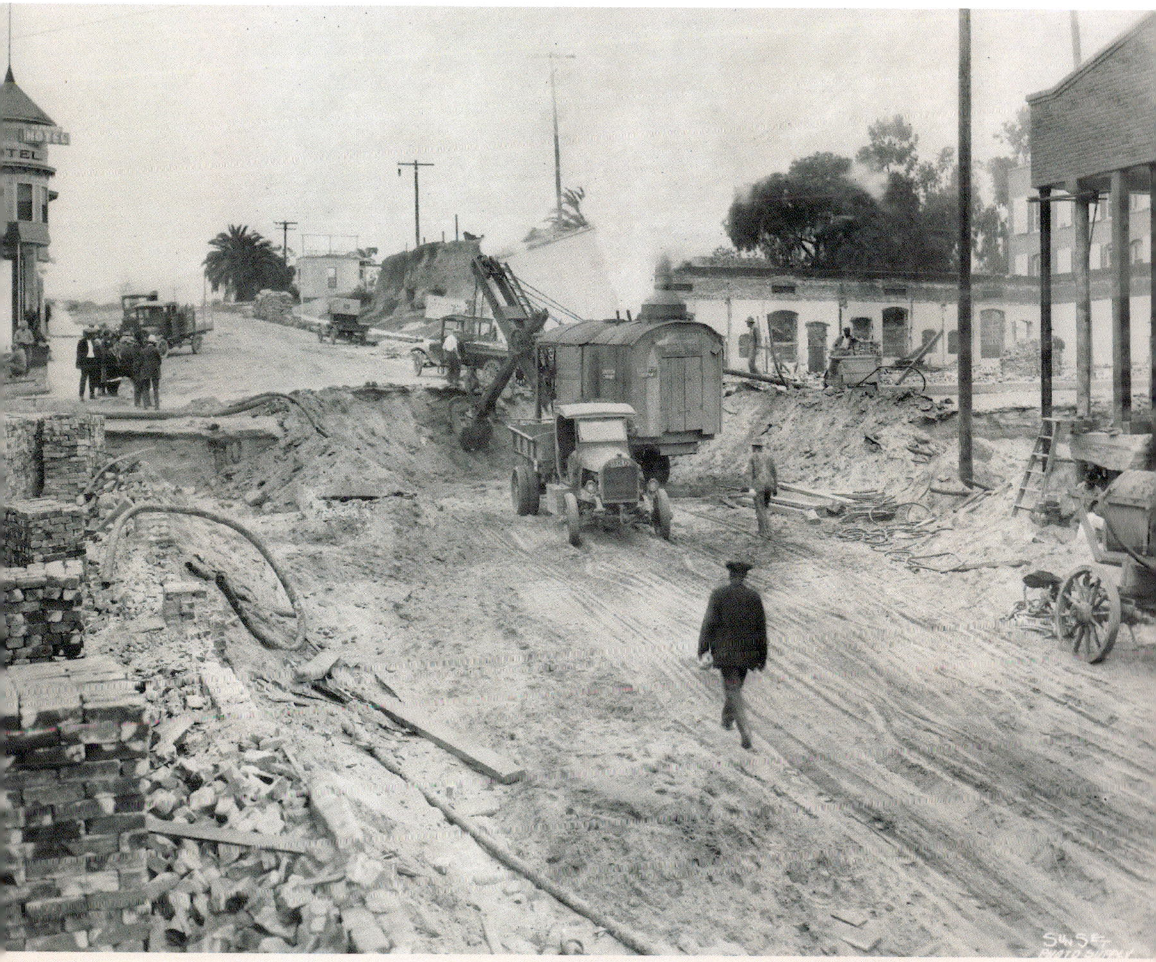

This is an early 20th century view—looking north on Fifth Street—of workers lowering the elevation of that street between Palos Verdes and Centre Streets. The Saint Francis Hotel (left) would eventually be propped up on wooden ties. A photograph of this project further along at this location can be viewed in chapter four.

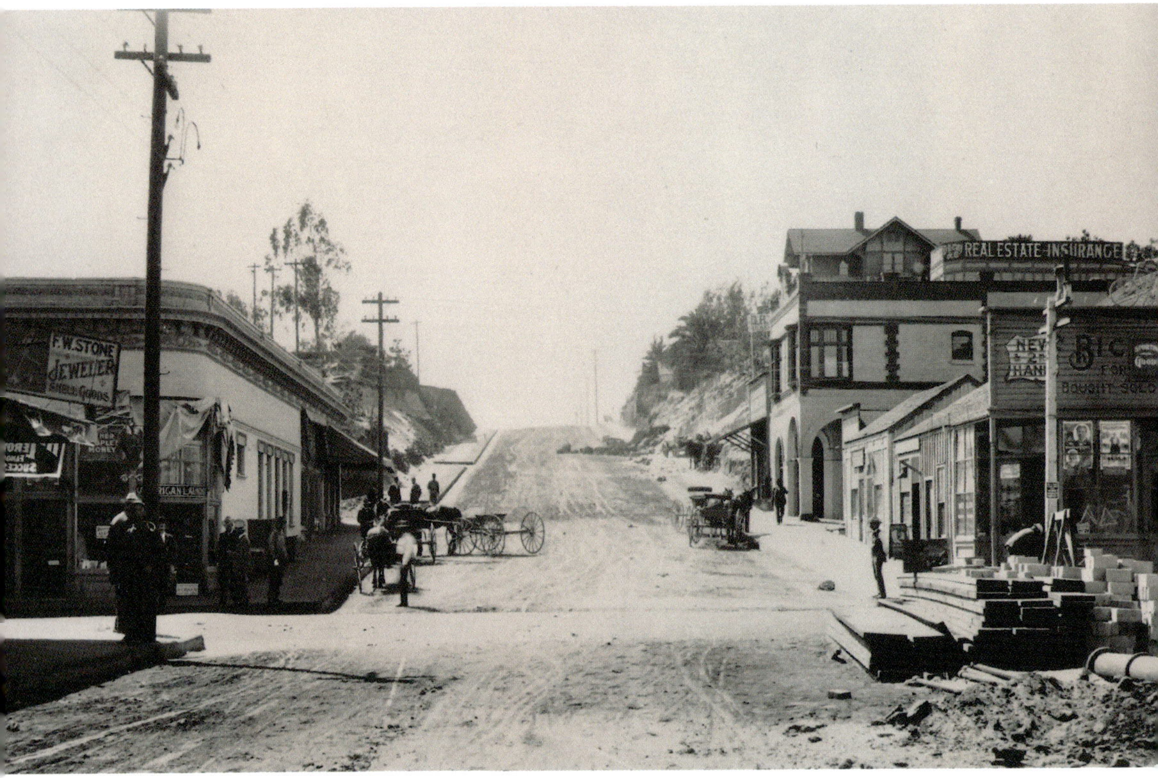

The 1902 photograph above shows Beacon Street looking south across Sixth Street. The top portion of the Dodson house and D. R. Clay and Company Real Estate (which are located on Seventh Street) can be seen in the upper left. That section of Seventh Street was much higher than Beacon. The white building with arches on the right of the photograph is George H. Peck and Company. The contemporary photograph below shows the municipal building (left) on Seventh Street. A Mexican restaurant is now located where a bicycle shop was located in the vintage image. Peck's office and other buildings on that side of the block are now parking lots.

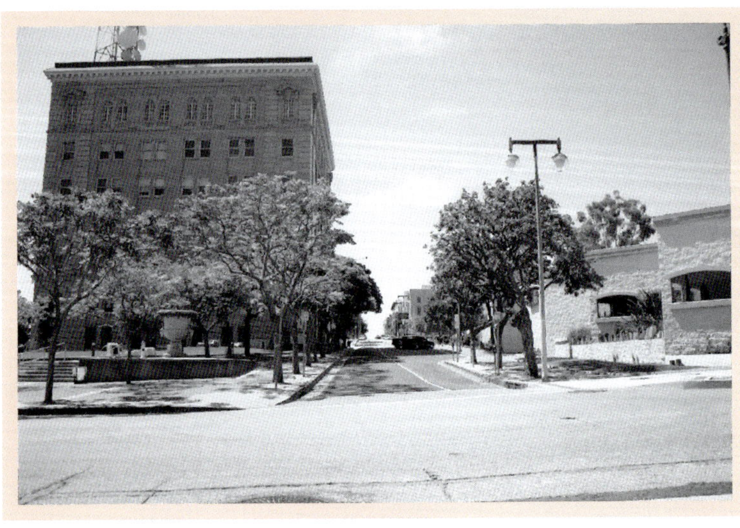

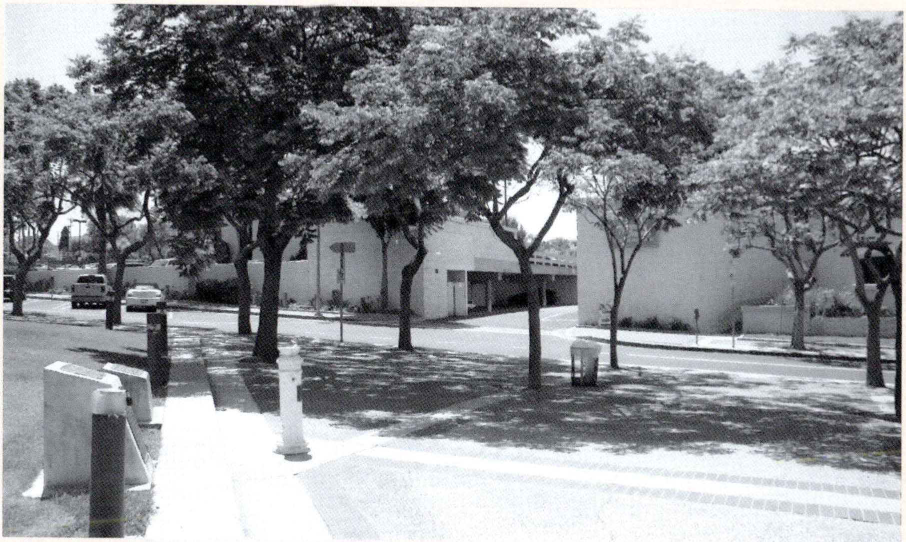

George H. Peck (1856–1940) was a major landowner and developer in San Pedro. He also owned land in Manhattan Beach. Pictured below in a pre-1920s photograph is Peck sitting in his automobile parked in front of the George H. Peck Real Estate office, which was located between Sixth and Seventh Streets on Beacon Street. The large map in the office window is now on display at the San Pedro Bay Historical Society. Today a parking lot occupies that site, and street parking is metered.

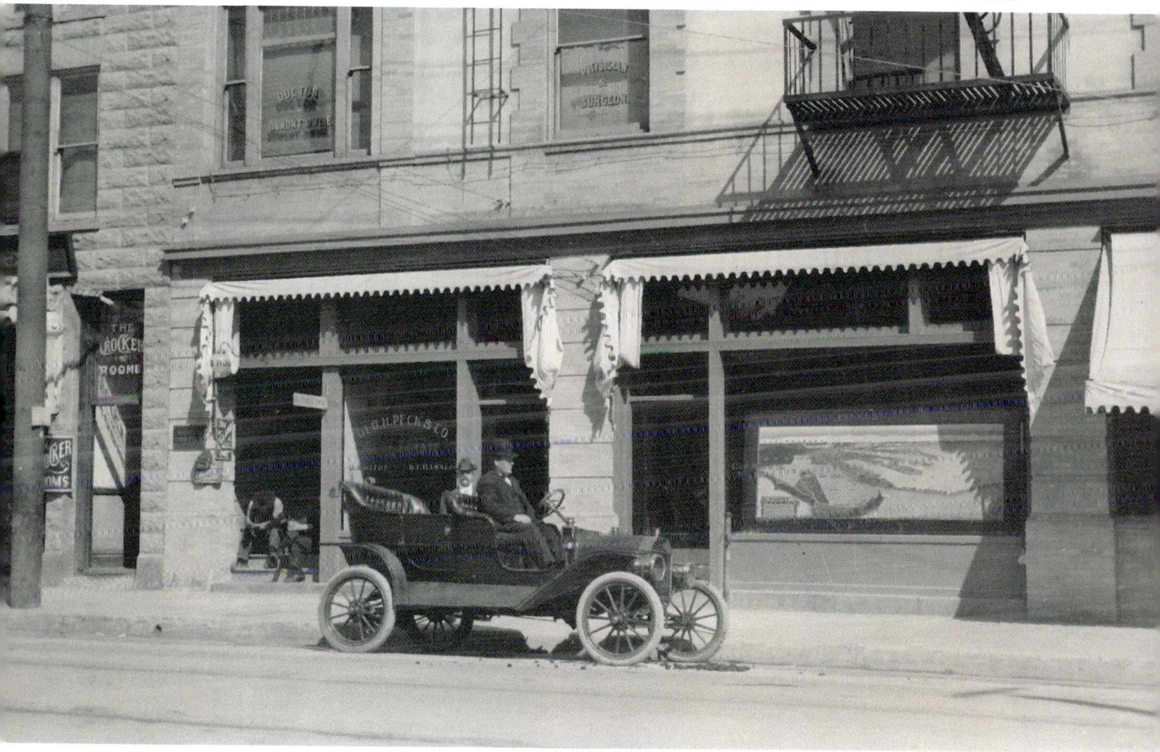

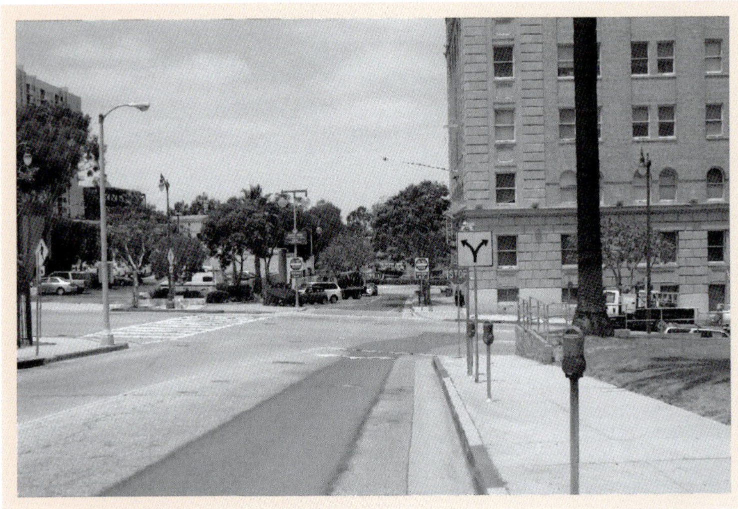

The intersection of Beacon and Seventh Streets is probably one of the most recognized areas of San Pedro. Historical structures—such as the Dodson house, the Fox Cabrillo Theatre, the A. P. Ferl building, and a city hall—have been located at that intersection. The vintage photograph below, taken about 1909 or 1910, is looking north on Beacon Street across Seventh Street. On the right is San Pedro's new city hall. Since Los Angeles incorporated San Pedro in late 1909, its function as a city hall was short-lived. The A. P. Ferl building on the left has been occupied by a number of businesses ranging from a music store to a marine technical bookstore. The vintage photograph was taken when it was the San Pedro Emergency Hospital. Today on the site of the Ferl building is a parking lot. City hall was demolished and replaced with a seven-story municipal building in 1928, which is still a functioning city building.

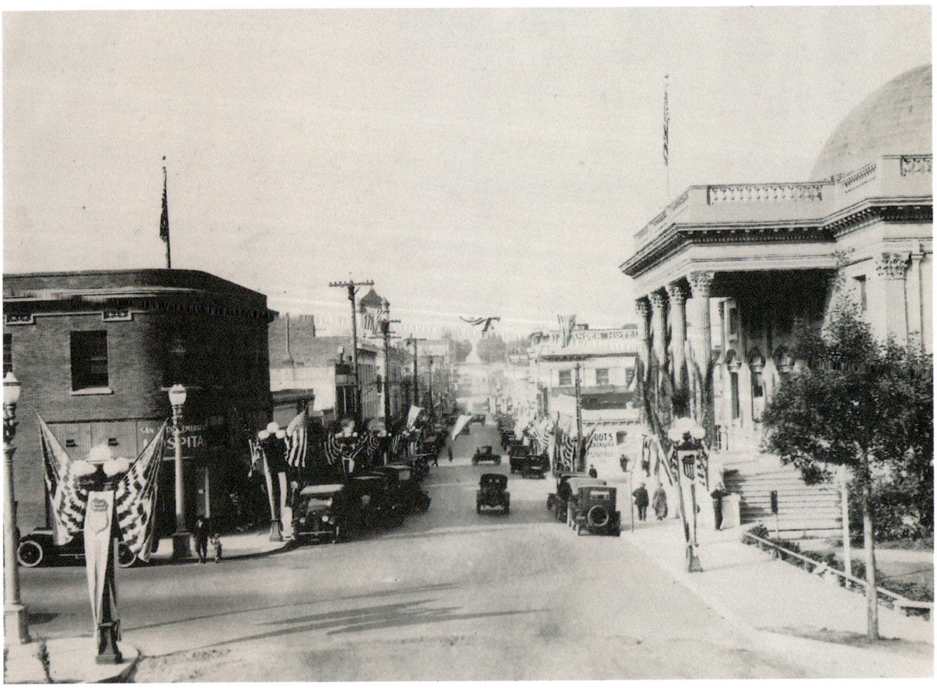

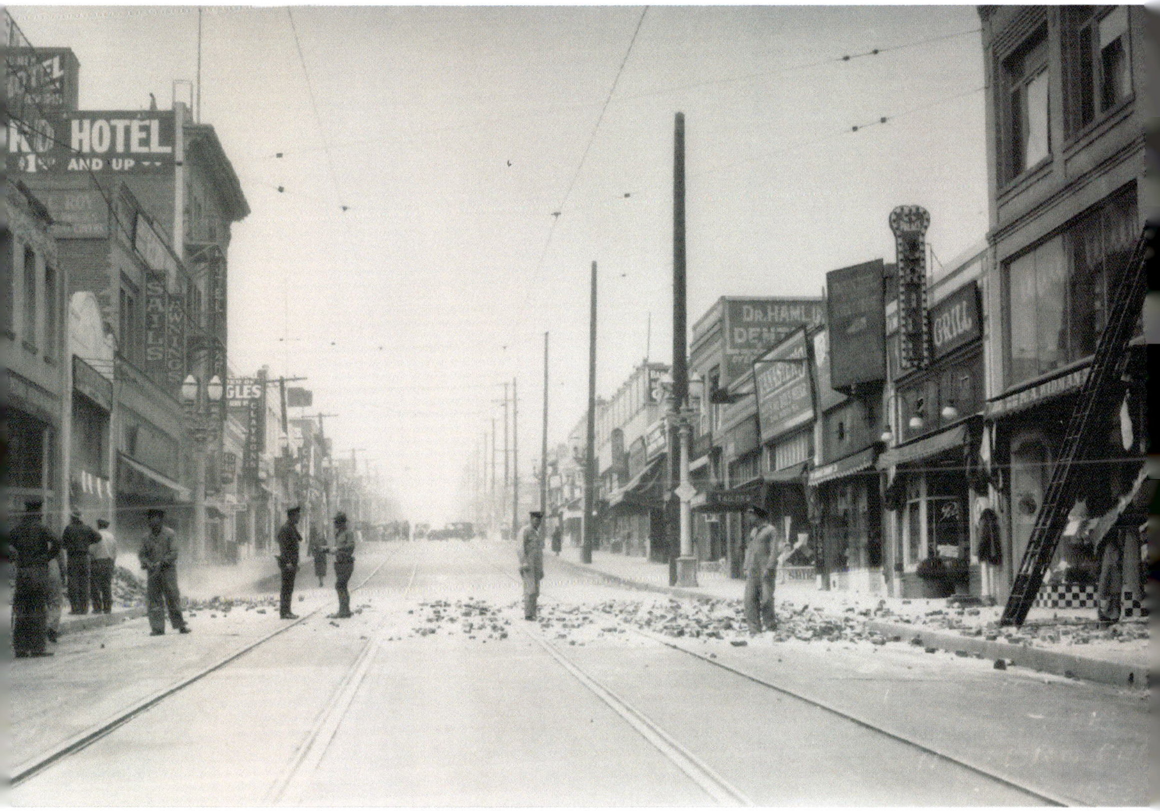

On March 10, 1933, at 5:55 p.m., San Pedro was struck by what would become known as the Long Beach earthquake. The 1933 photograph above is looking west on Sixth Street near Palos Verdes Street. The Hotel Oxford on the left, which offered daily room rates from $1 and up, did not sustain much exterior damage. Workmen are clearing away major debris while a policeman and an army officer have a discussion in the street. All buildings in the vintage photograph have been demolished. The Crowne Plaza Hotel and Resort (left) and Northrop Grumman now dominate that location.

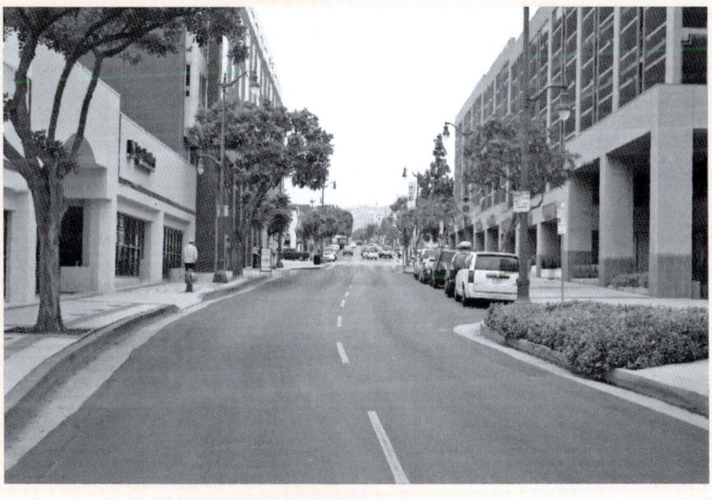

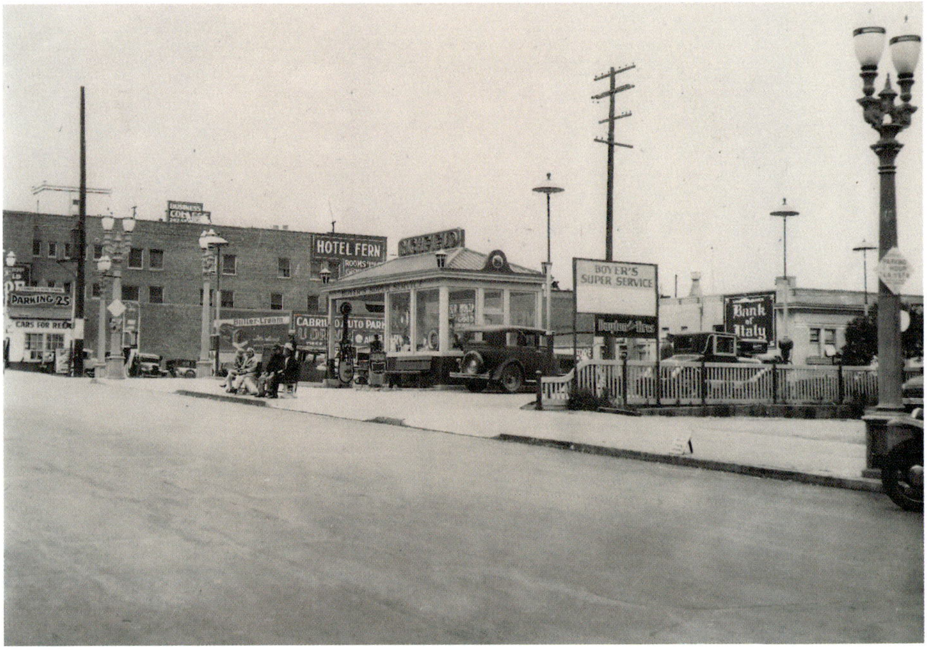

Standing on the northeast corner of Seventh and Palos Verdes Streets was a Richfield gas station, as seen in the center of the 1930 photograph above. In the background is the rear of the Hotel Fern. The back wall of the Bank of Italy (now known as Bank of America) building is on the far right. Both were on West Sixth Street. The Crowne Plaza Hotel (formerly the Sheraton Hotel) now takes up that entire block. A city of Los Angeles facility is now where the gas station was located. After the many years that have passed since the 1930 photograph was taken, a bus stop still remains on that corner.

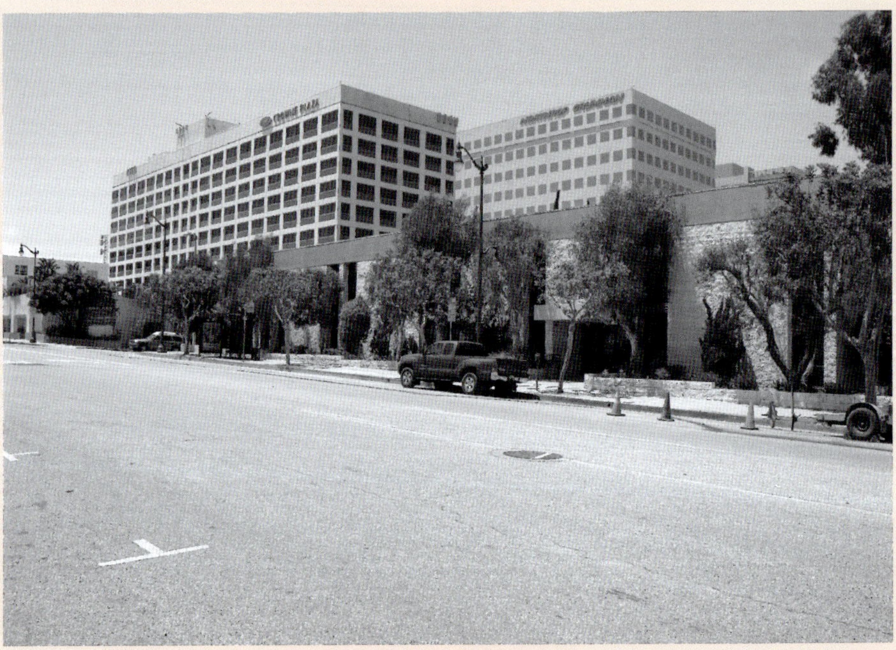

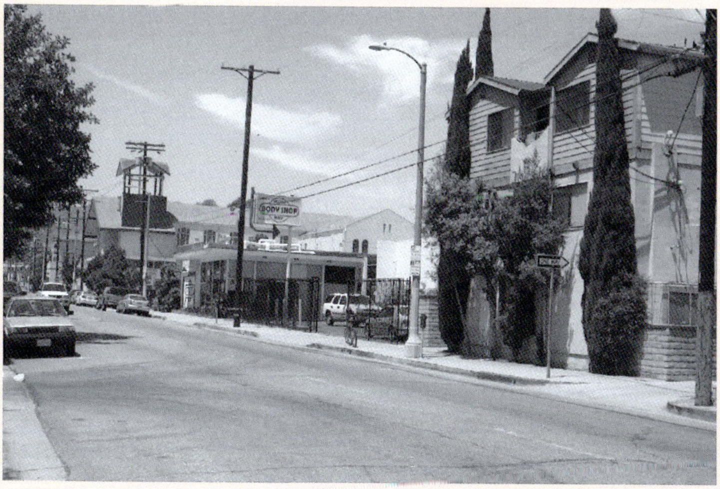

In the early 1960s, teenagers—probably from San Pedro High School—held a fund-raising car wash on the south side of Sixth Street near Pacific Avenue. In the upper left corner of the *then* image below is San Pedro First Methodist Episcopal Church. East (right) of the church are Halverson Mortuary and M and M Body Shop. Farther down the street, where the men are standing, was a union hall. In the present-day photograph above, the church (now named San Pedro United Methodist Church) and the building of M and M Body Shop (now South Bay Body Shop) are still standing. The Halverson property is now a playground for the church. Other buildings in the car wash photograph have been demolished. The parking lot where the *then* photograph was taken is now the site of a building.

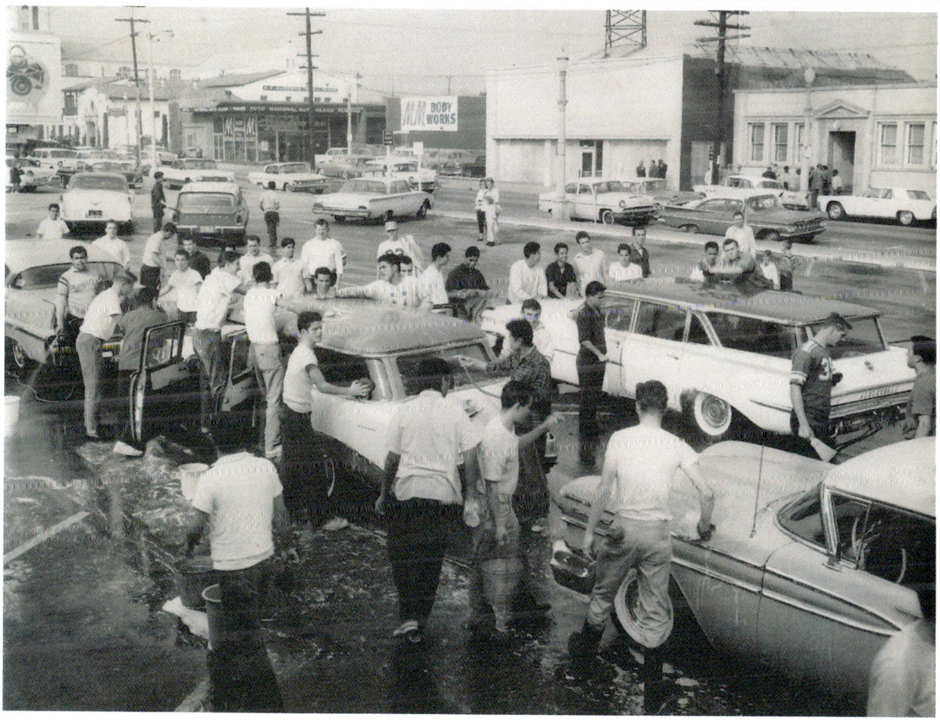

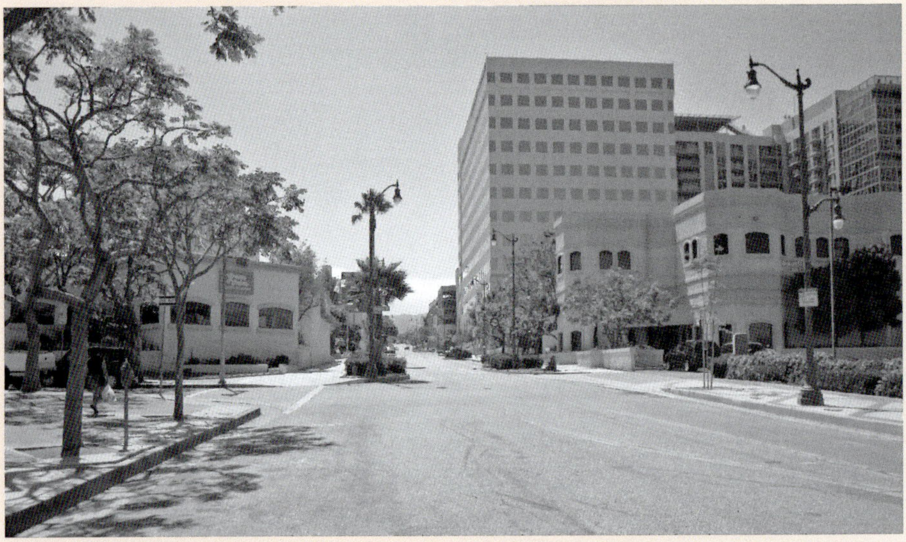

Many of San Pedro's historical buildings were still standing in the late 1960s at Sixth and Beacons Streets. The *c.* 1969 photograph below is a view of Sixth Street looking west across Beacon Street. The old Bank of San Pedro building in the right foreground was the bank café at the time. The north wall of the Anderson building is on the corner across the street. These, and other buildings in the area, were demolished as part of the Beacon Street Redevelopment Project in the early 1970s. The present-day photograph above shows an office building (right), Northrop Grumman, and a parking structure occupying that property. The Green Onion Mexican Restaurant and the Crowne Plaza Hotel and Resort (formerly the Sheraton Hotel) are now on the property across the street.

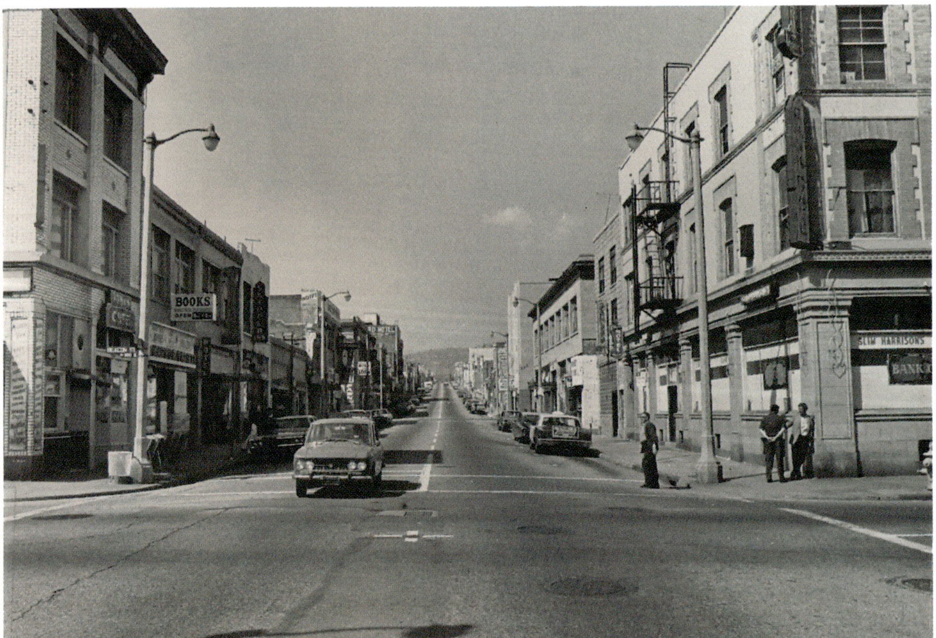

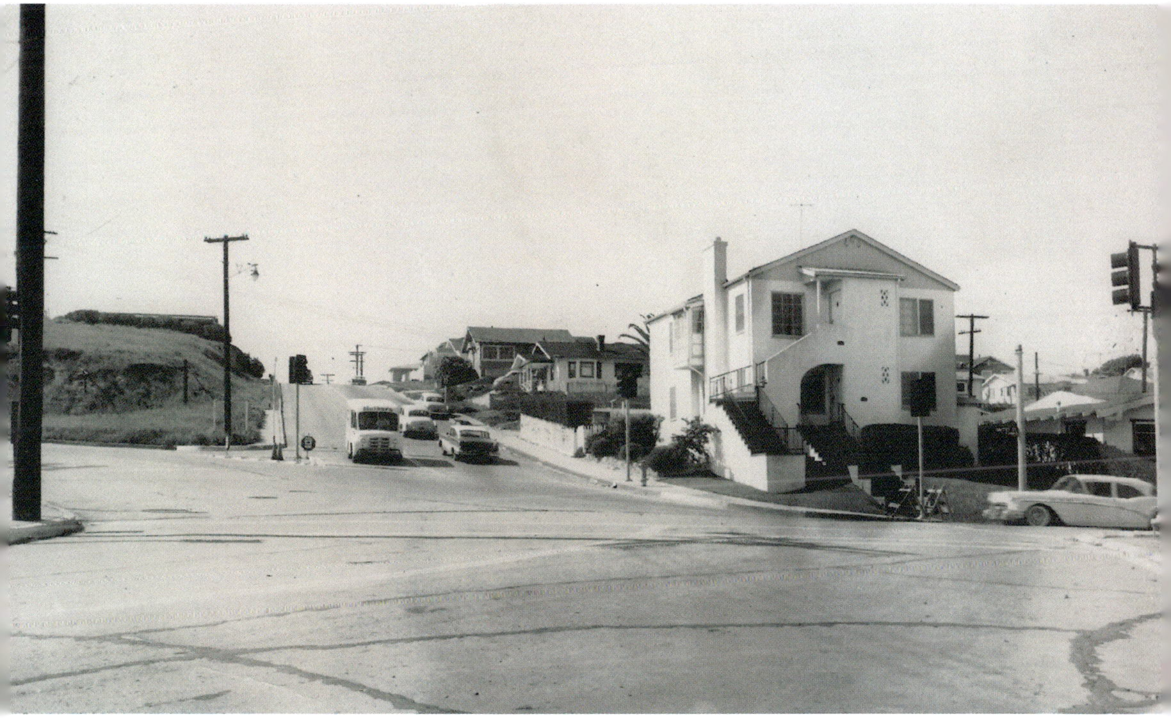

Located near the highest point of South Gaffey Street is the intersection of Twenty-fifth and Gaffey Streets. The *c.* 1950s photograph above is looking west across Gaffey Street to Twenty-fifth Street (center). It shows a different contour of the streets than the present-day intersection. Twenty-fifth Street was wider, and Hamilton Avenue (lower left of 1950s photograph) once fed into this intersection. The present-day photograph, taken from Hamilton Place across Gaffey Street, shows that Twenty-fifth Street has been slightly narrowed at this point when the sidewalk was widened. Hamilton Avenue has been cut off from the intersection, as seen in the lower right corner of the contemporary photograph. The house on the northwest corner remains, but other structures have been demolished and replaced. Multiple-family dwellings now occupy the vacant land seen in the earlier photograph.

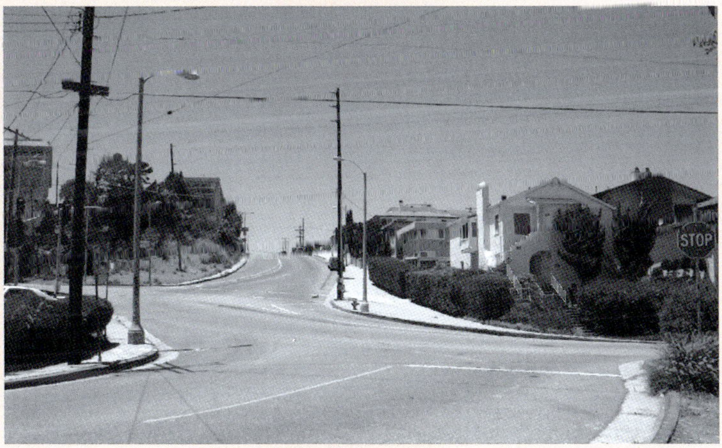

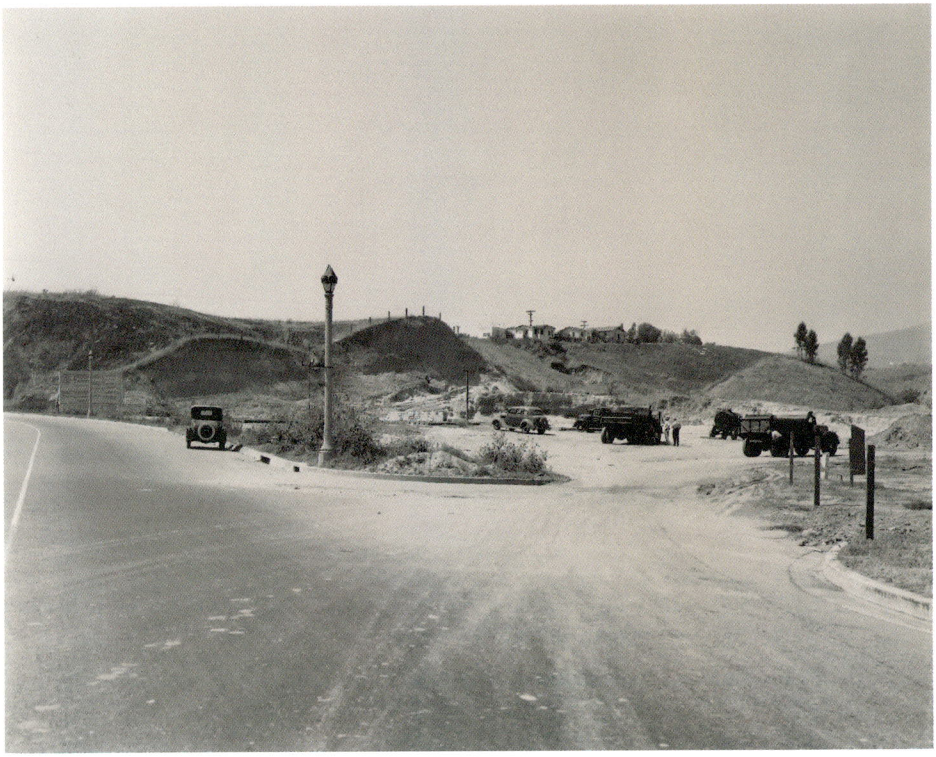

The intersection of North Gaffey and Miraflores Streets had yet to be developed in the *c.* 1930 photograph above. Hills on the left are the northern section of what is now Leland Park. Small businesses, such as a car wash, are now on the site where vehicles are parked in the vintage photograph. On the right is the new home of Fire Station No. 36. It opened in November 2007. For years, this station was located in the municipal building.

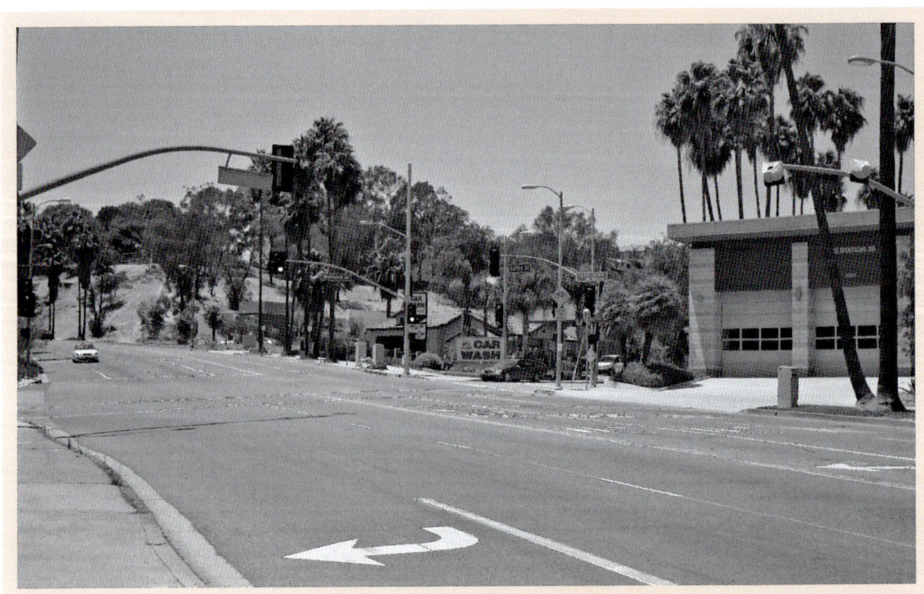

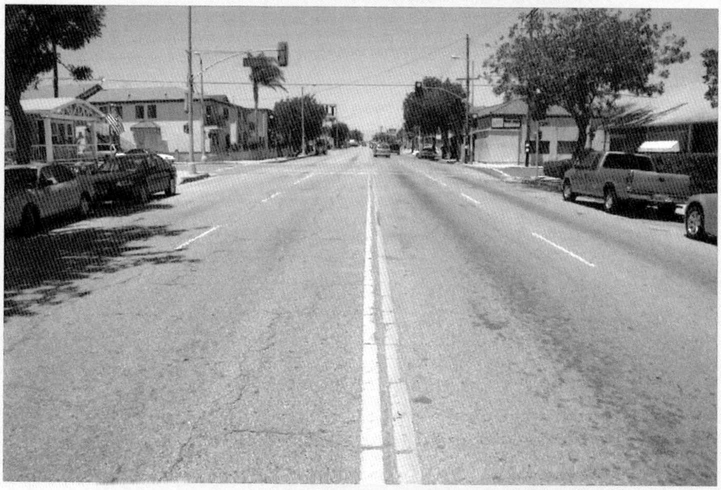

A photographer used an 8-by-10-inch view camera to take the below photograph of South Gaffey Street looking north in the late 1920s or early 1930s. It shows how streets were illuminated at night at the time. A string of lights supported by cement columns hangs over the center of Gaffey Street. The name of the first building on the right may reflect the economic mood of the time: Western Cash Grocery. The present-day intersection has traffic lights, and the grocery store building has been replaced, along with many of the single-family residences that appear in the vintage photograph.

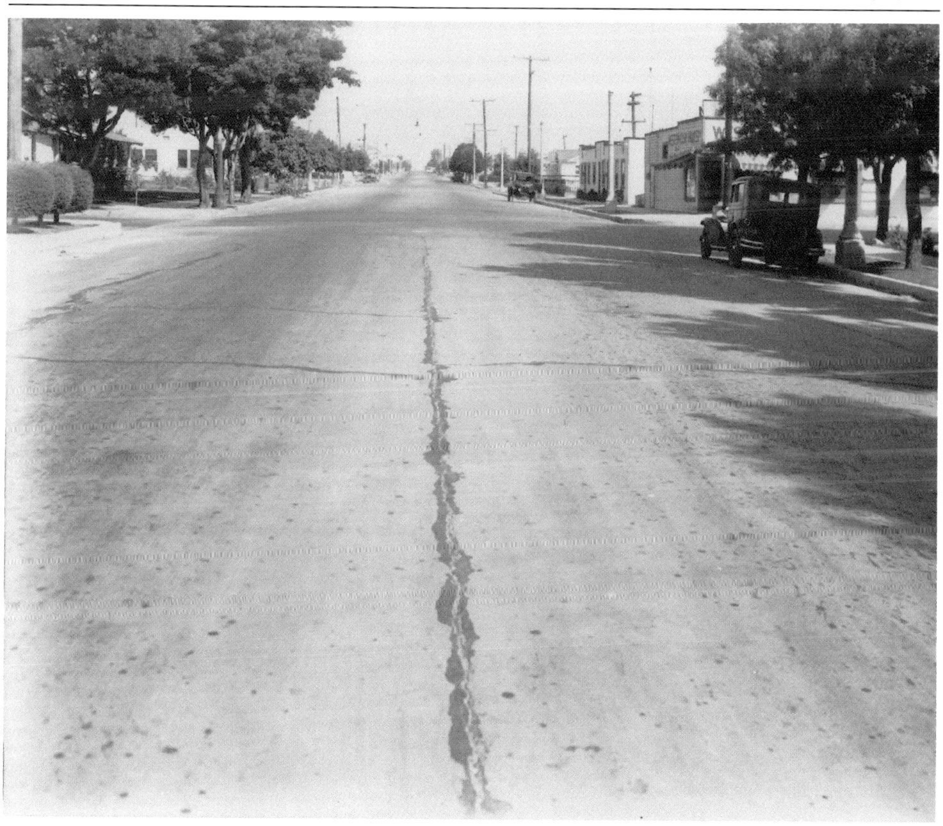

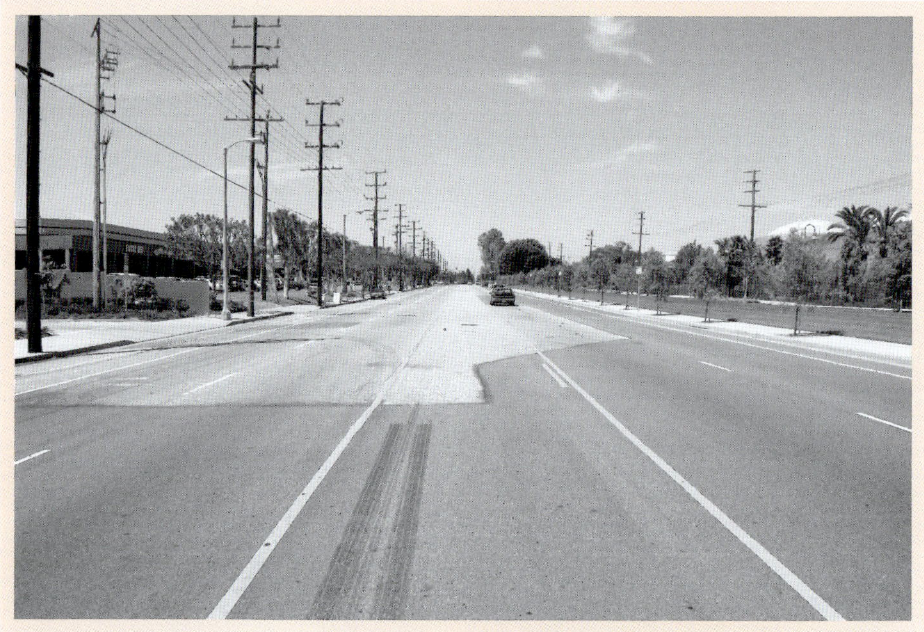

The undated photograph below shows North Gaffey Street flooded. The San Pedro drive-in (left) was located at 1811 North Gaffey Street and opened June 6, 1949. On the right side of the street is a billboard for Vic Tanny Health Clubs. The Vic Tanny gyms were popular in the 1950s to late 1960s. They were forerunners of today's health club industry. In the present-day photograph above, there is a narrow park/walkway (right). A public storage facility and other small businesses are on land once occupied by the drive-in theater. The building on the far left is approximately where the theater's iconic screen was located.

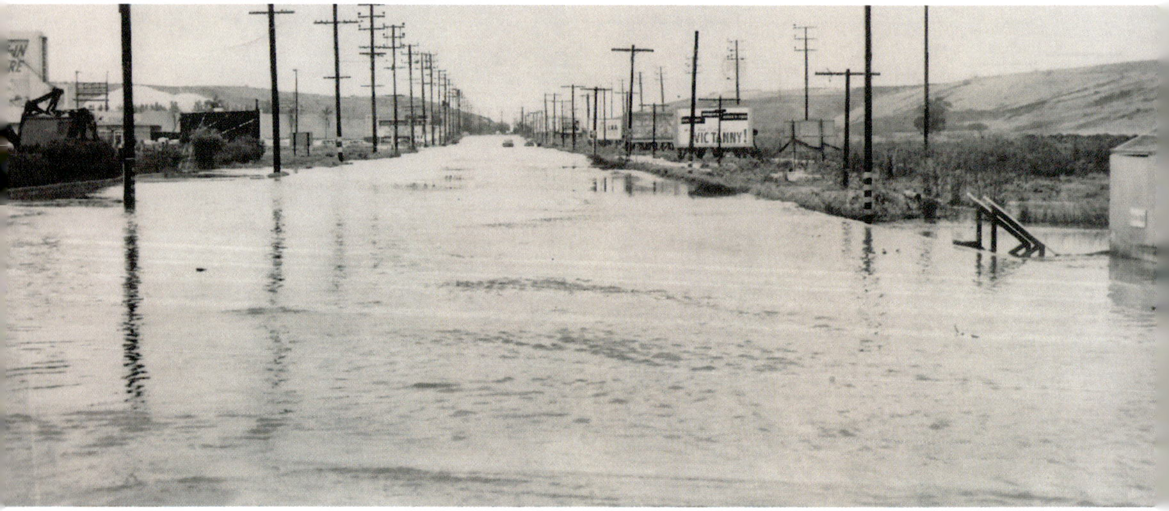

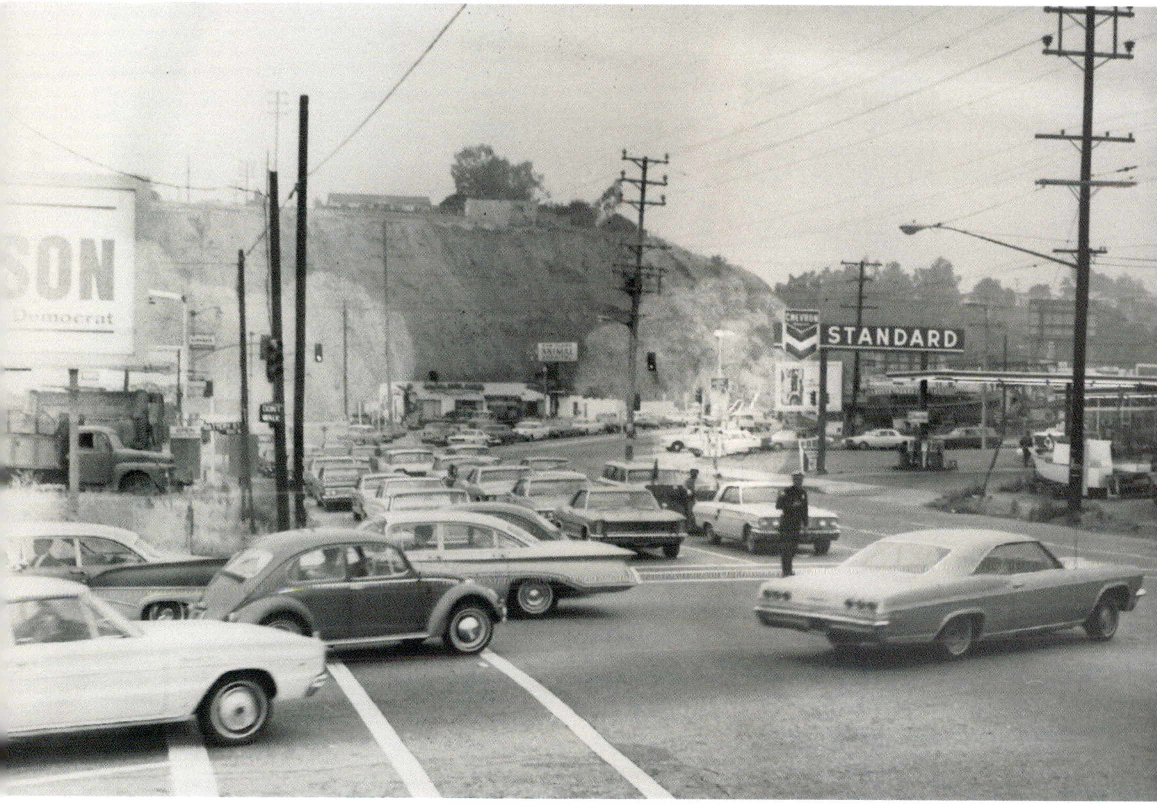

Taken while facing south from the intersection of Battery and North Gaffey Streets in the late 1960s, the photograph above shows Battery Street when it was a busy thoroughfare. A Los Angeles traffic policeman is standing in the intersection and directing traffic. Battery Street has since been cut off to through traffic because of construction of the Harbor (110) Freeway, but the Chevron gas station on the right is still in business. Traffic signals in the background are at Channel and Miraflores Streets. The hills of the northern section of Leland Park are in the background of both photographs.

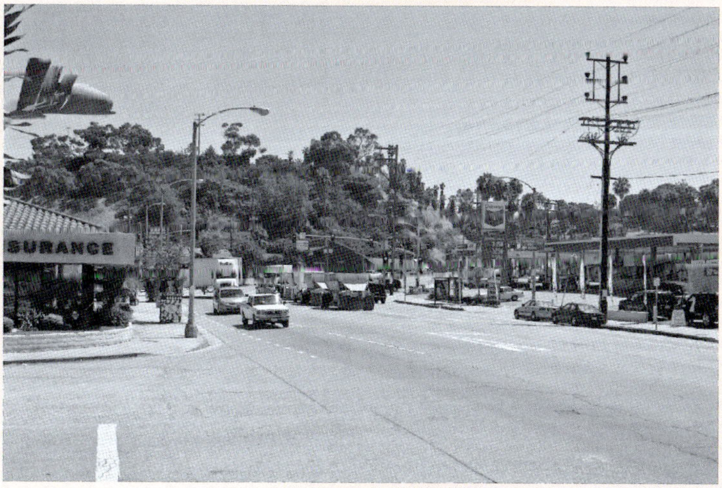

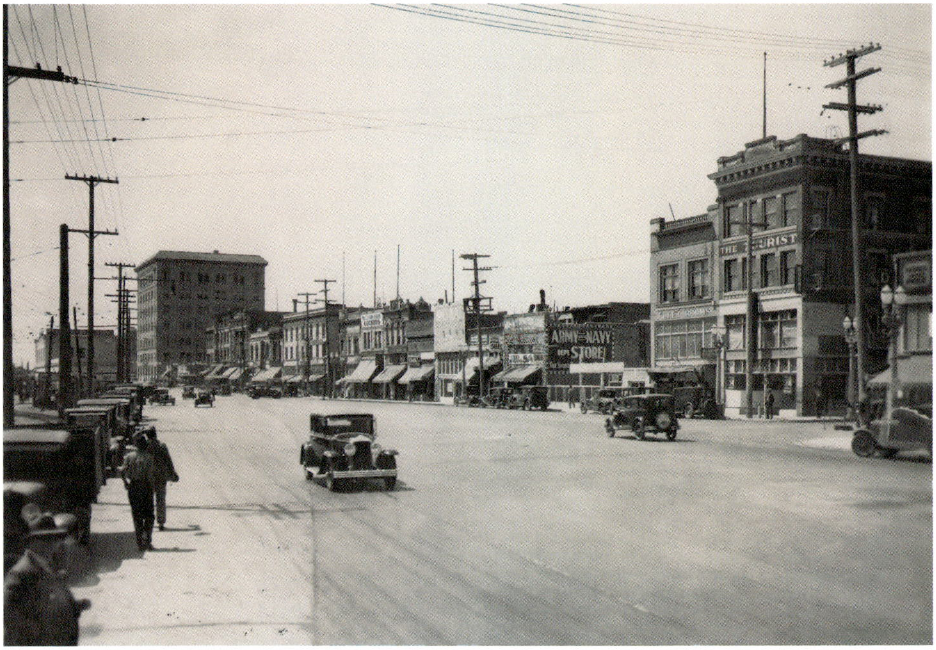

Harbor Boulevard (formerly Front Street) in the 1930 photograph above seems relatively quiet the year after the Great Crash of 1929. Taken while facing south from Fourth Street, there are many businesses that catered to sailors, commercial fishermen, and related occupations. To the right of the municipal building is the eastern entrance of the Hotel Alexander on Sixth Street and Harbor Boulevard. The dome of the former Carnegie Library can barely be seen to the immediate left of the municipal building. Today the block between Sixth and Fifth Streets is mostly occupied by the Sunrise Hotel.

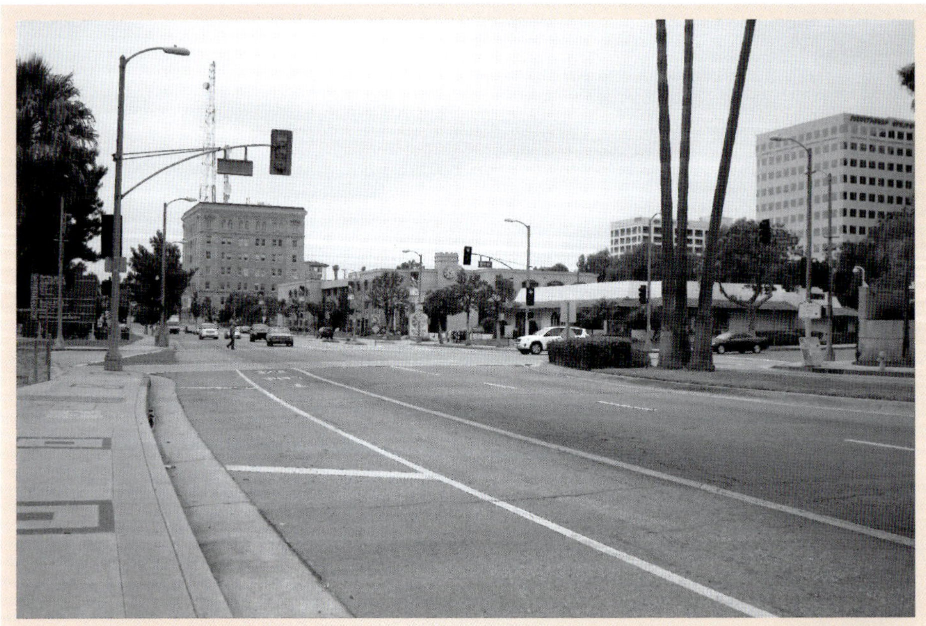

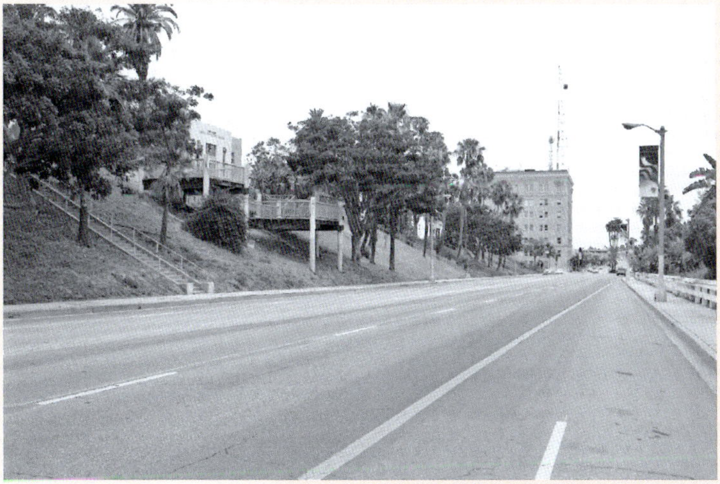

Construction of San Pedro's municipal building had not been completed in the photograph below taken on April 19, 1928 facing north on Harbor Boulevard (formerly Front Street). The domed building (left) housed the Carnegie Library from 1906 to 1924. From 1924 until it was demolished in the mid-1960s, it was the San Pedro Chamber of Commerce. The municipal building remains a functioning facility of the city of Los Angeles. The Maritime Industry Memorial is where the Carnegie Library once served the San Pedro community.

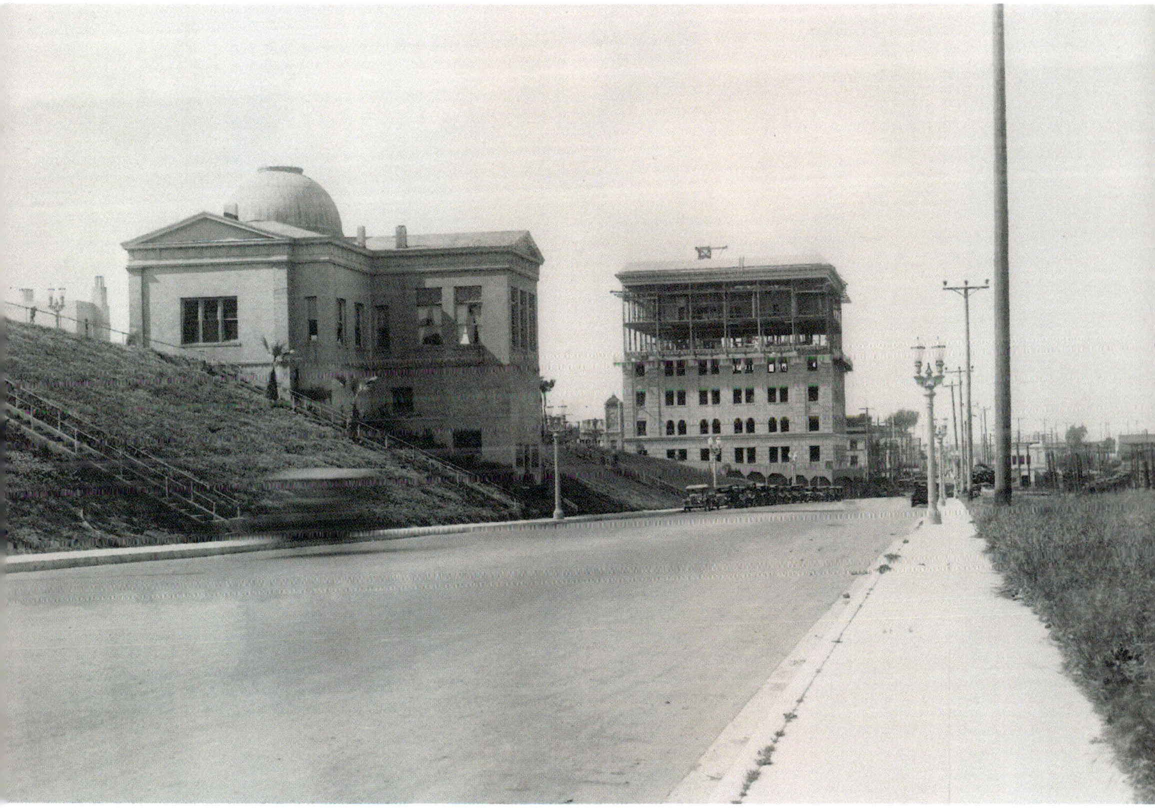

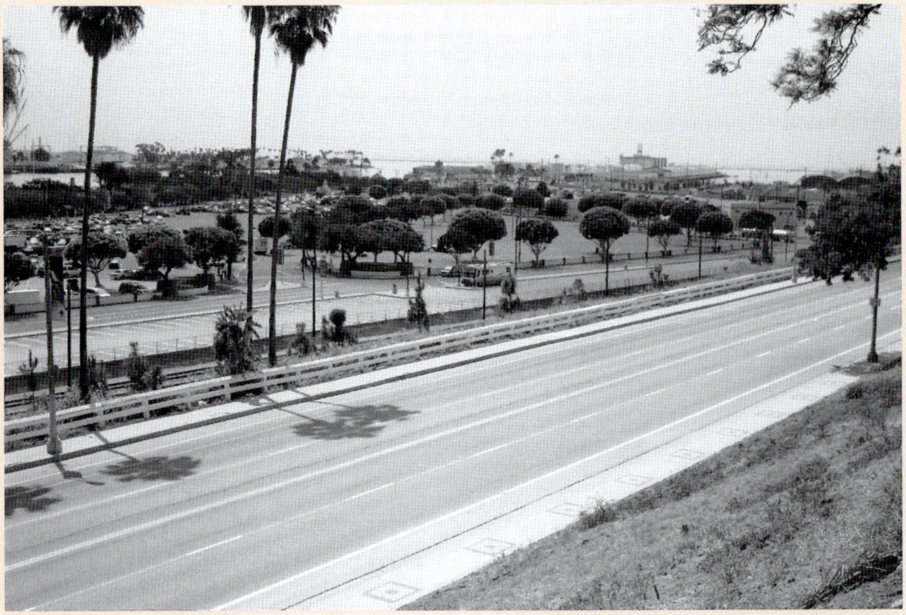

The 1961 photograph below is a southeastern view of Harbor Boulevard (formerly Front Street) with Ports O' Call in the background. In the far background is Warehouse No. 1. The only major tourist attraction at that time was the restaurant on the far left next to the white tanks. The present-day photograph shows that the water tower on the far right of the 1961 image has been dismantled. Warehouse No.1, which is listed on the National Register of Historic Places, still stands. The restaurant has been joined by a number of small tourist businesses, and some of the tanks have been removed. Parking is no longer permitted on most of the west side of Harbor Boulevard.

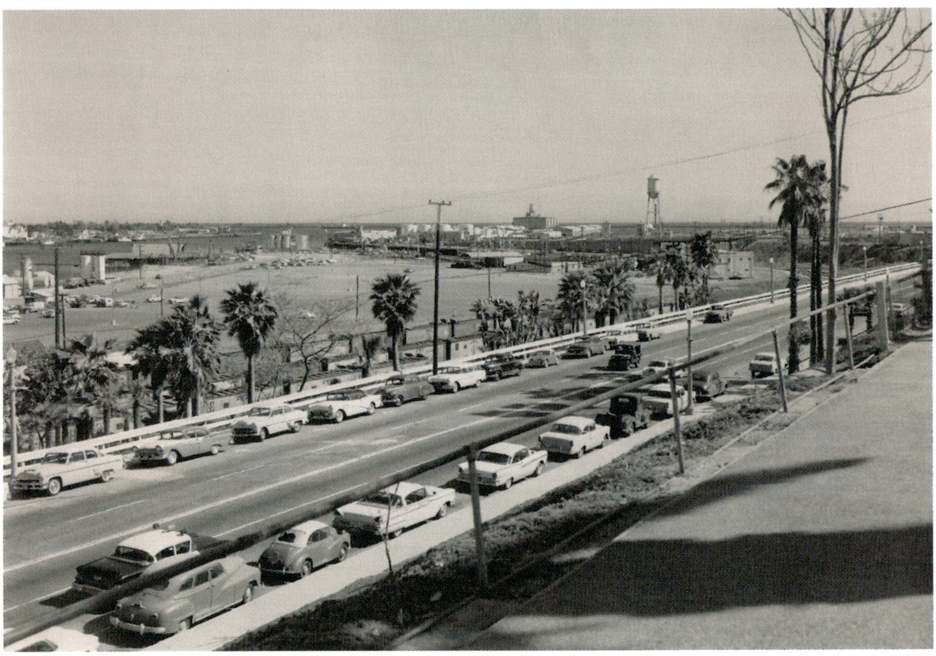

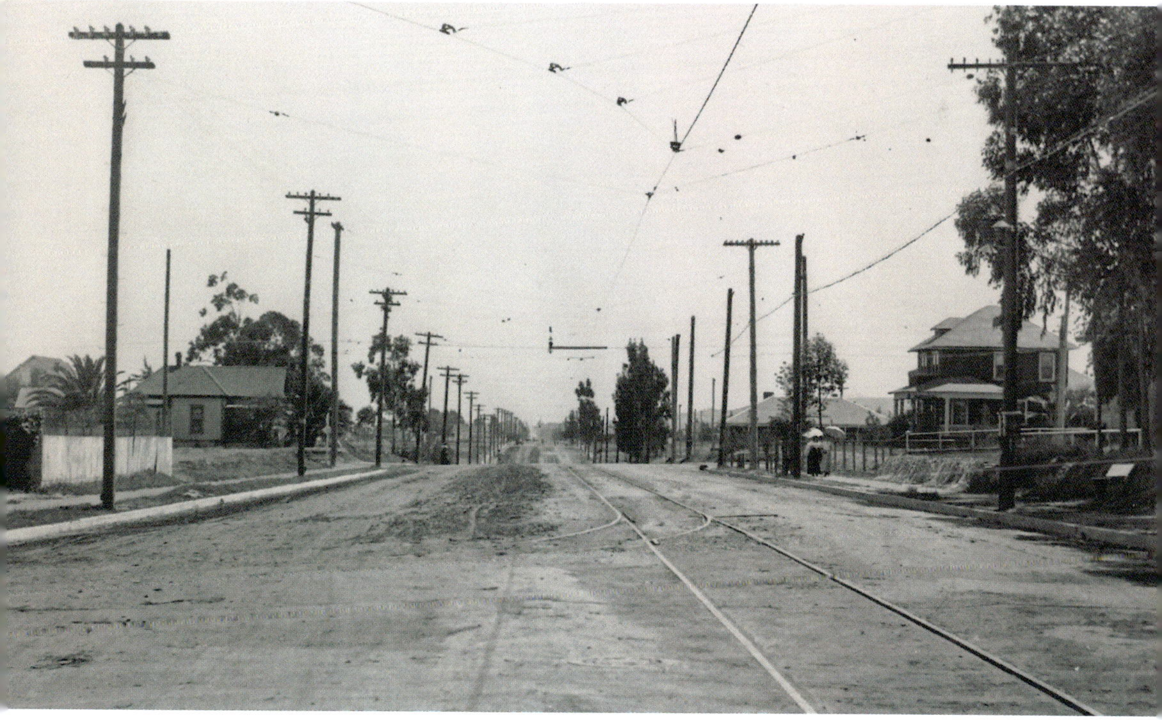

In 1912, a photographer took the above photograph of Pacific Avenue looking south from Sixth Street. Wires above the street show that electric streetcar service was available. The curved tracks and wires are coming from Sixth Street. The present-day Pacific Avenue and Sixth Street intersection is paved and very busy. The corner building on the left was once a JCPenney department store. Farther down, on the northeast corner of Seventh Street and Pacific Avenue (next set of traffic lights), was the S. H. Kress and Company 5-10-25c Store.

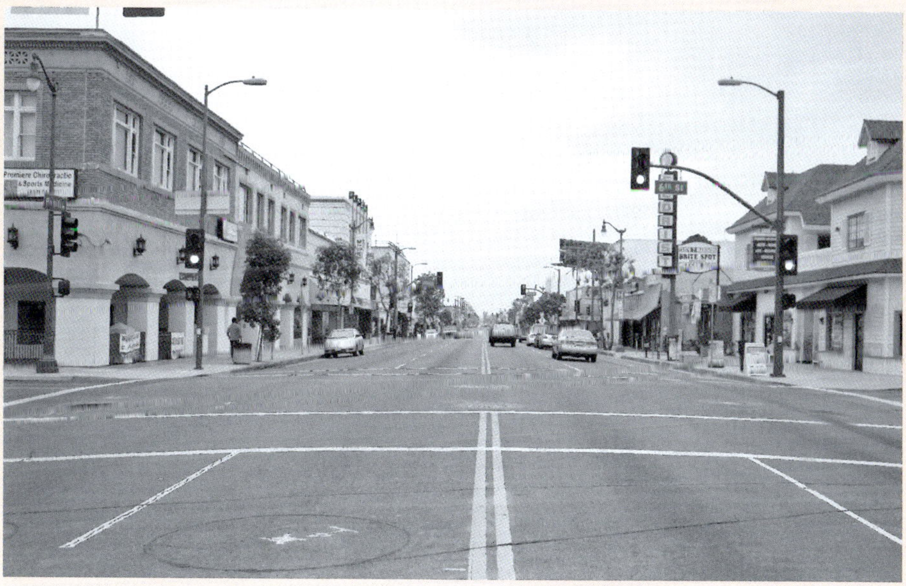

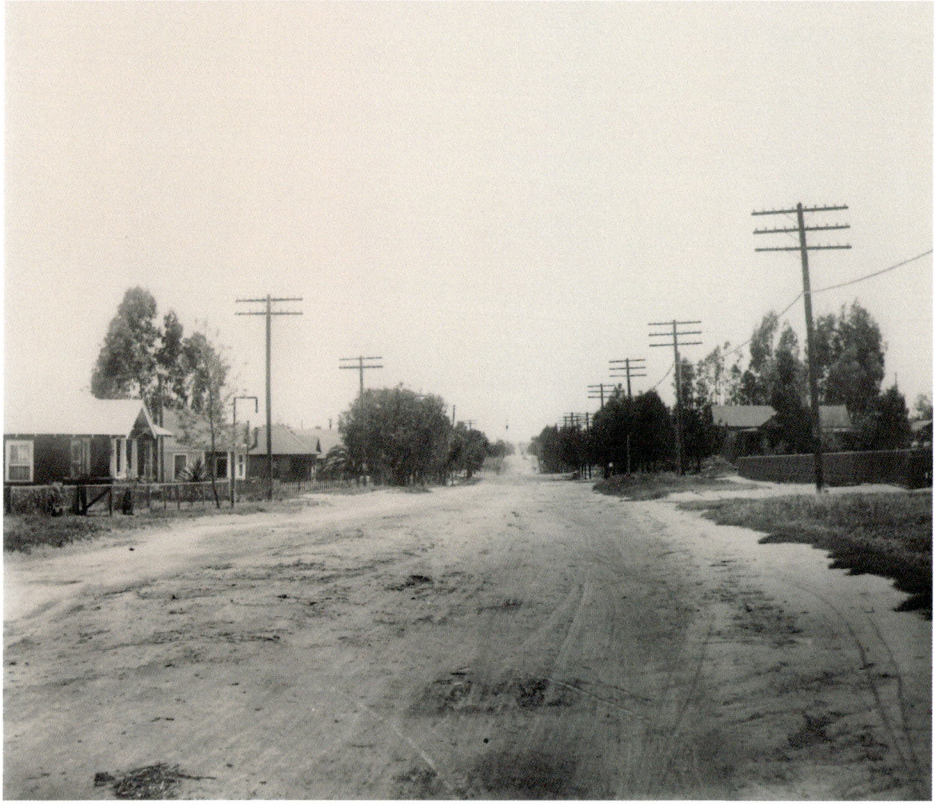

The 1912 photograph above, probably taken by the same photographer of the image on the previous page, shows what Pacific Avenue looked like facing south from Barton Hill School. Residences are on both sides of the street, which was not paved and had no sidewalks. Streetcar service was not available.

Today, as seen from the intersection of O'Farrell Street and Pacific Avenue, all the small houses have been replaced with commercial buildings. Barton Hill School is located at this intersection. A public bus system provides transportation along this street.

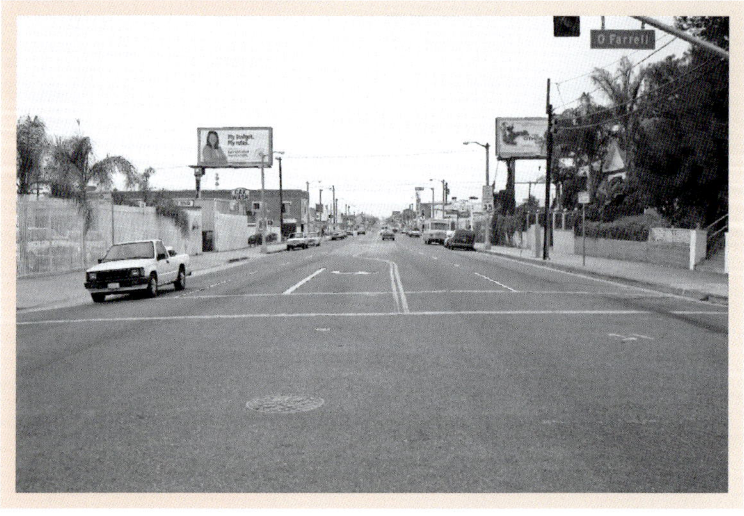

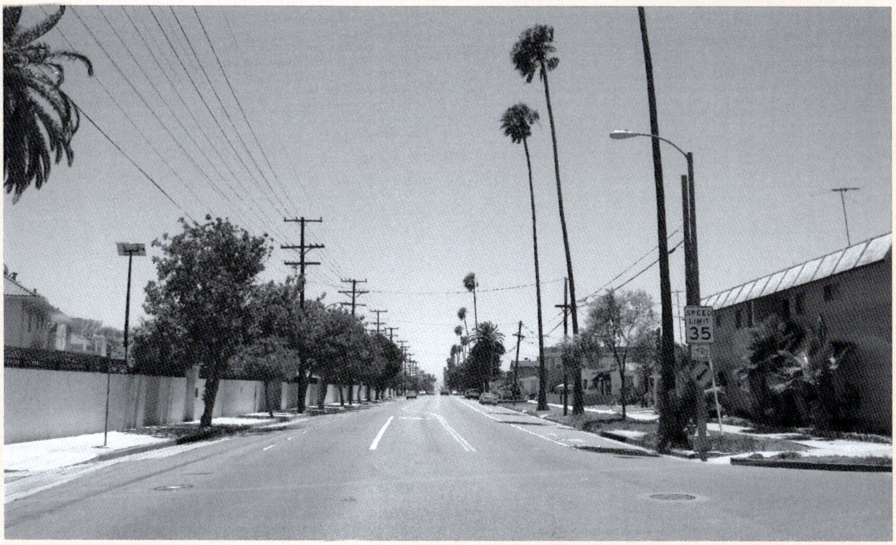

On August 15, 1916, a photographer took the image below of South Pacific Avenue facing south from Twenty-sixth Street. Construction of the streetcar track had not yet been completed. A merchant's horse-drawn wagon is parked on the left, next to the grounds of Fort MacArthur (an active army post from 1914 to 1974). The present-day view above shows the left wall that surrounds Fort MacArthur (left), which now provides housing for the air force, and private housing on the right. No evidence of the once busy streetcar service remains.

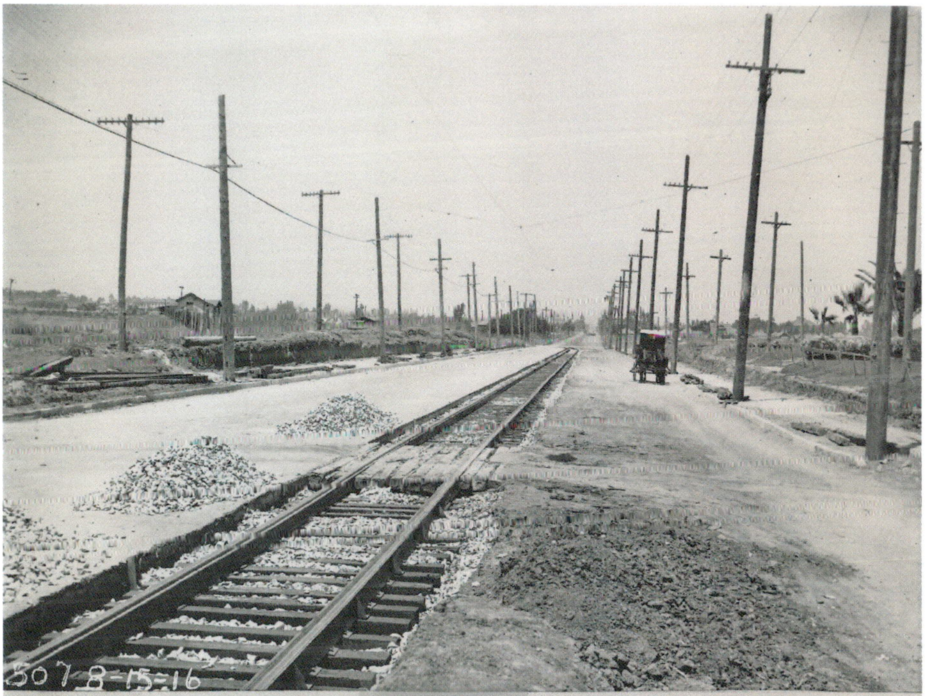

AUGUST 15, 1916 - LOOKING SOUTH ALONG PACIFIC AVENUE (SAN PEDRO) FROM 26th STREET. (negative reversed)

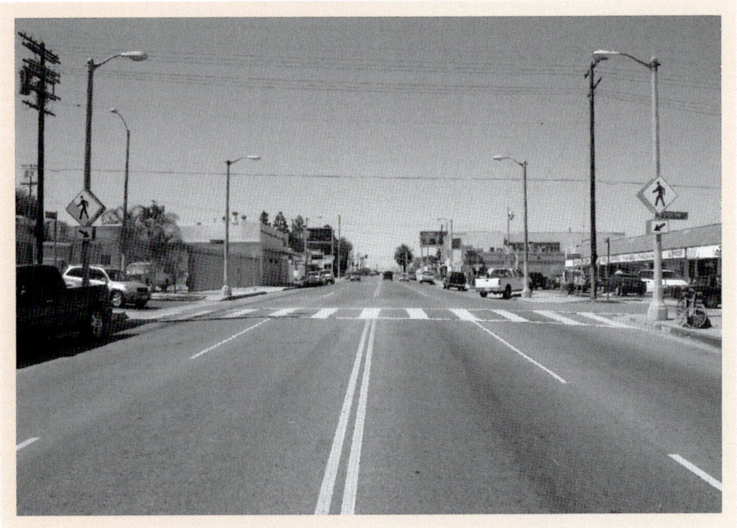

Looking north on South Pacific Avenue across Santa Cruz Street in the 1930s (below) is very different from the present-day view. Then, one would have seen the marquee of the Barton Theater on the left. In the far background on the left side of the street is the roof of Barton Hill Elementary School. Today the Barton Theater is gone. An automobile repair shop and parking lot are now on that property. Barton Hill Elementary School is still at the same location (a building obscures the view of the school). A mini mall now occupies the land on the right were there once stood an apartment building and a low billboard.

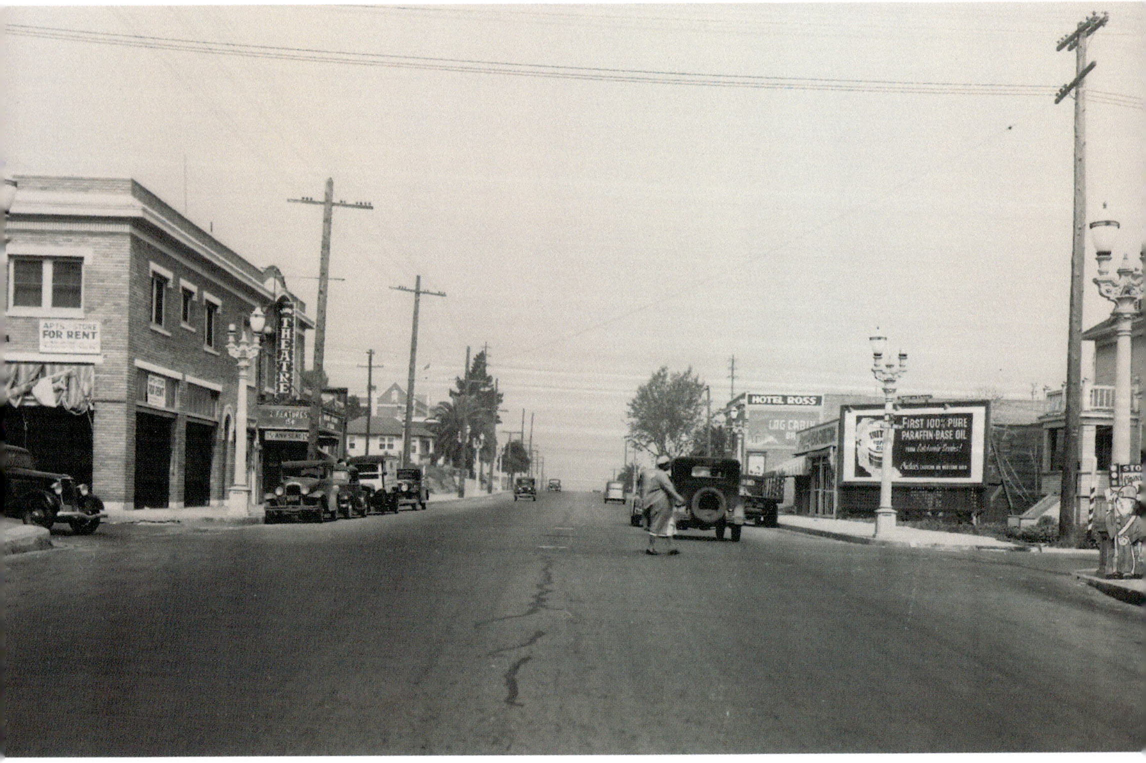

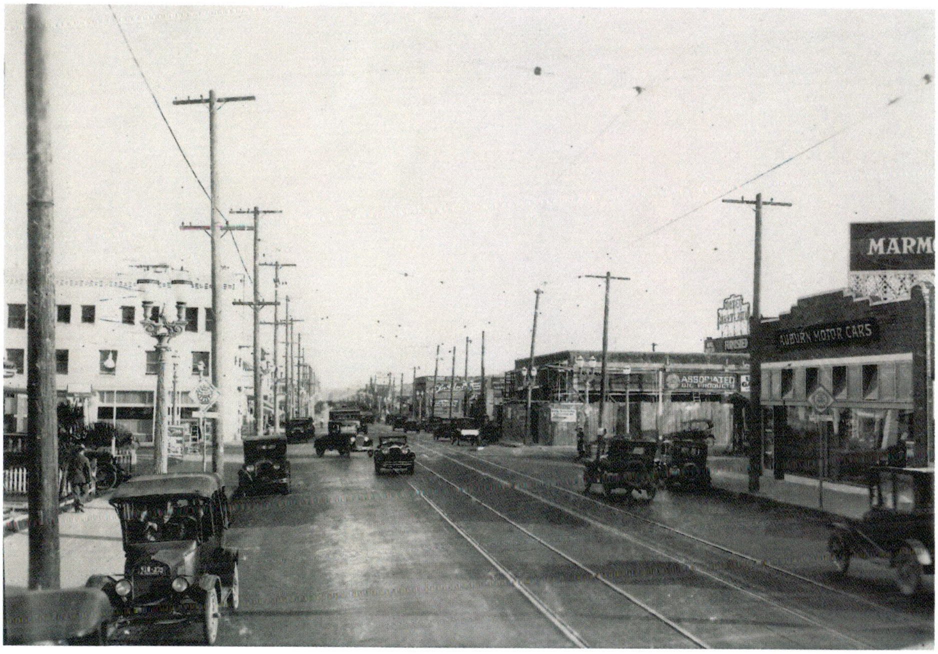

By the late 1920s, South Pacific Avenue was well on its way to becoming an important area of commerce, as seen in the 1927 photograph above. Taken while facing south on Pacific Avenue from Sixth Street is Auburn Motor Cars, a gas station, and a building being renovated by Foss Designing and Building Company on the right. Farther down the right side of the street is the insurance company of M. L. Campbell and Son. The large sign of the Maryland Hotel can be seen to the left of Auburn Motor Cars. It is located on West Eighth Street. Some of these structures have survived. The building that housed the car company has been remodeled. The gas station site is now the Croatian Cultural Center of Greater Los Angeles (formerly a bank building constructed in 1928). The M. L. Campbell and Son insurance building still stands but now houses small businesses and apartments. The Maryland Hotel remains in business.

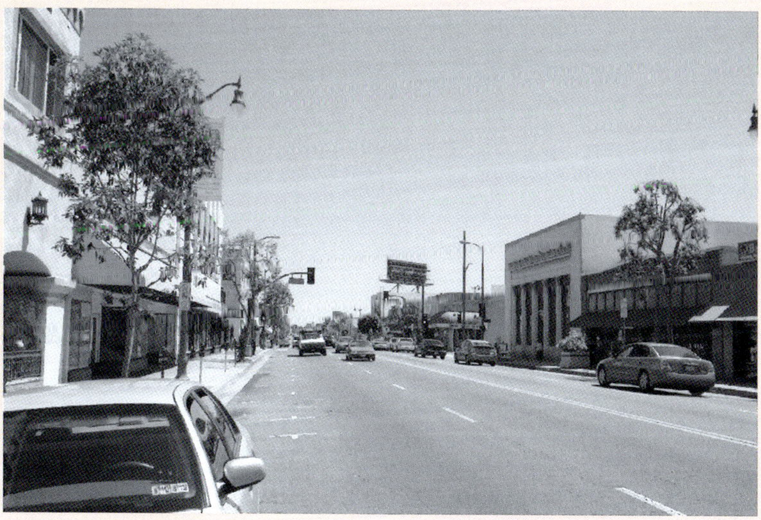

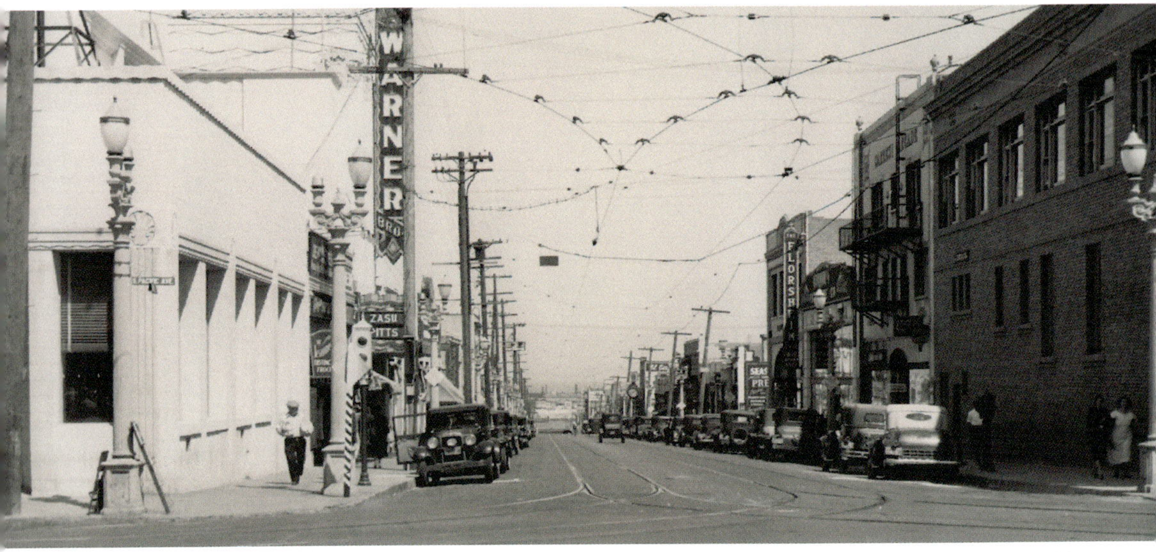

Judging by the number of parked automobiles in the above *c.* 1934 photograph of Sixth Street facing east across Pacific Avenue, businesses seemed to be doing relatively well considering the country was about midway through the Great Depression. The art deco Warner Grand Theater (left) opened on January 20, 1931. The Brown Brothers building (Florsheim Shoes sign on the right) has been on that property since 1927. The Warner Grand is now owned and operated by the City of Los Angeles, and the Brown Brothers building (behind the tree on the right in the present-day photograph below) is home to a number of merchants. The intersection now has traffic signals, and the electrical wires and tracks for the streetcar service have long since been removed.

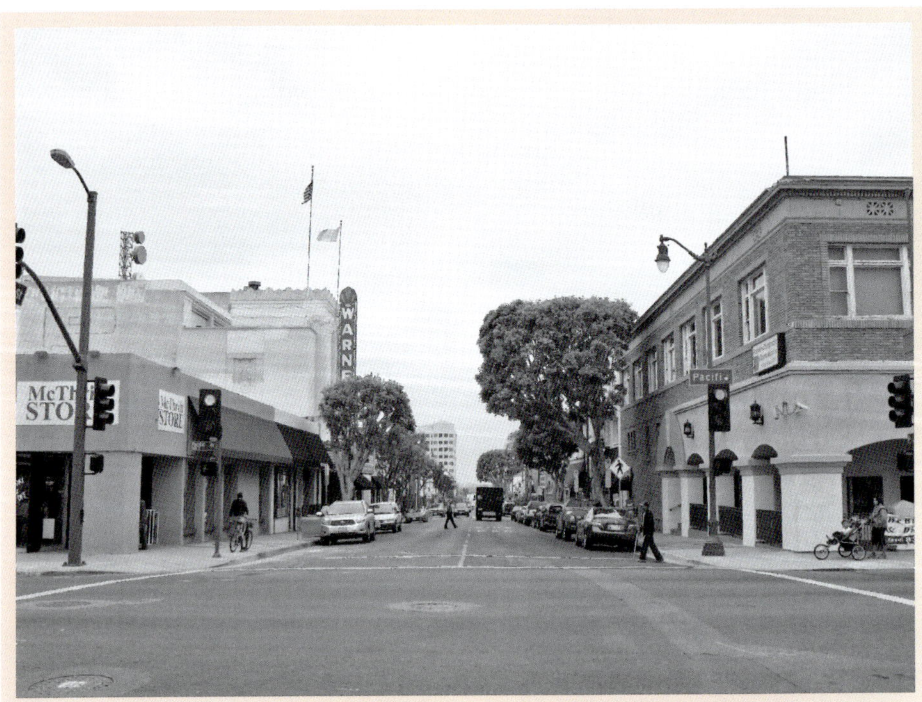

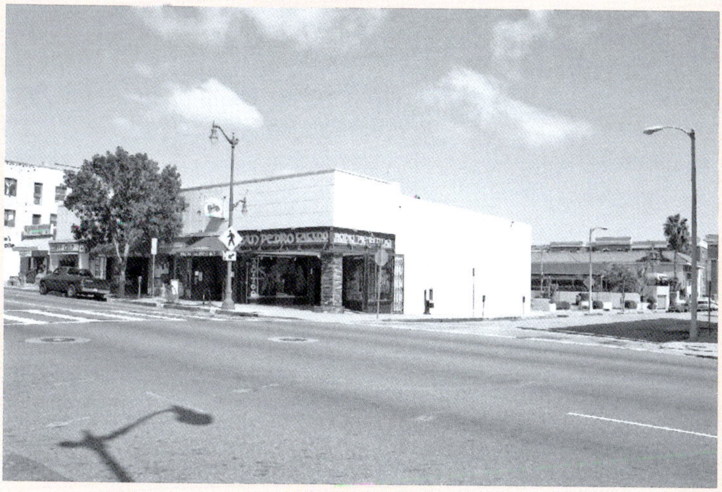

The Ruth Spere School of Dancing (and jazz piano lessons) was located on the northeast corner of Eighth Street and South Pacific Avenue, as seen on the far right of the *c.* 1930 photograph below. The automobiles on the right are parked on Eighth Street. The dwellings on Eighth Street have been replaced with commercial buildings, and the dancing school site is now the location of a tattoo and body-piercing parlor. The tall building on the other side of Spere continues to be a functioning structure on Pacific Avenue.

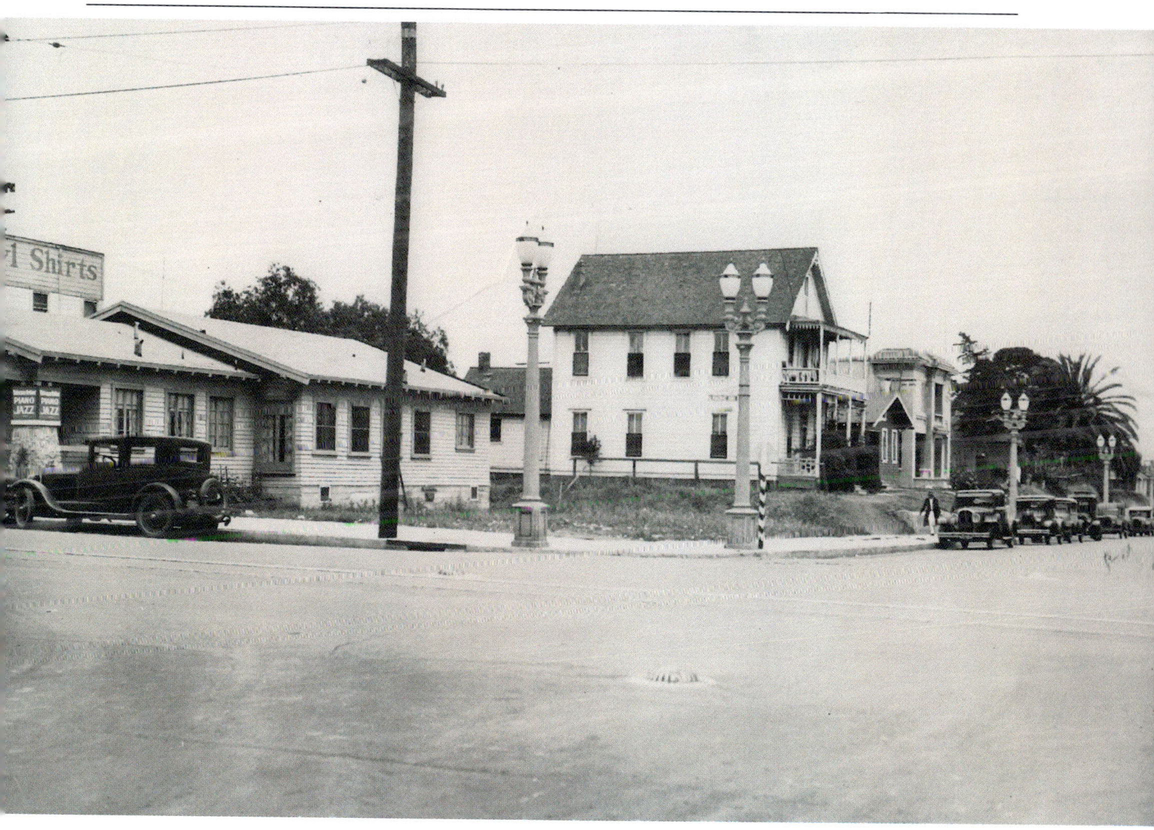

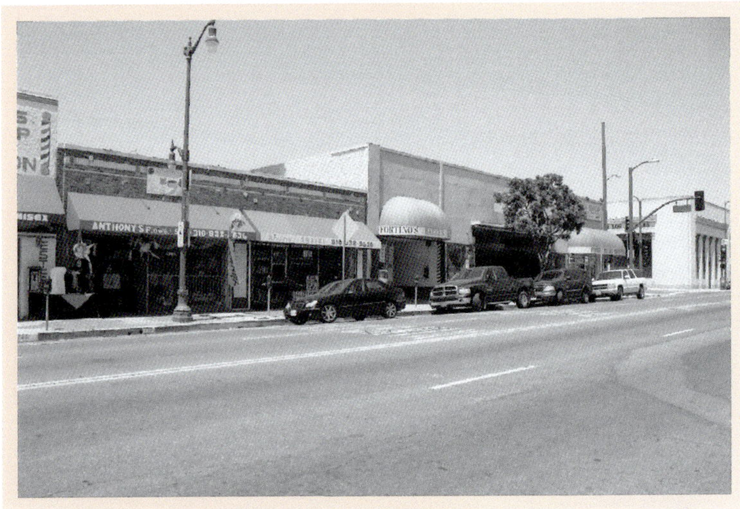

An annual event in San Pedro was the Cabrillo Day Parade on Pacific Avenue. Judging by the Cord 810 convertible automobiles in the photograph below, it shows possibly the 1936 or 1937 parade. The Cord was manufactured by Auburn Automobiles, and there was an Auburn dealership in San Pedro. Moving south on South Pacific Avenue just past Seventh Street, a Safeway Grocery can be seen under the large Red Lion billboard, as well as a boy under that sign who seems to be aware a photograph is being taken. The sign the boy is sitting on reads, "Old Gold Cigarettes—Not a Cough in a Carload." An Italian grocery store, a photography studio, and a café are on that part of the block. Across the street (right) is a bank. Businesses in the vintage photograph are gone, but the structures remain. The bank building is also still standing and is now the Croatian Cultural Center.

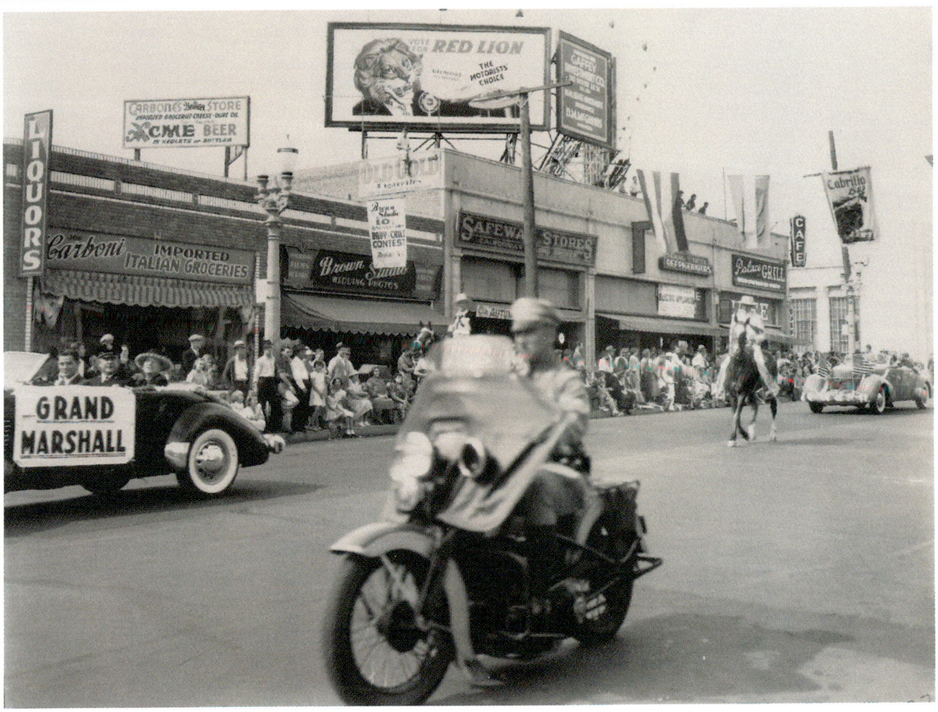

CHAPTER 3

Government and Municipal Sites

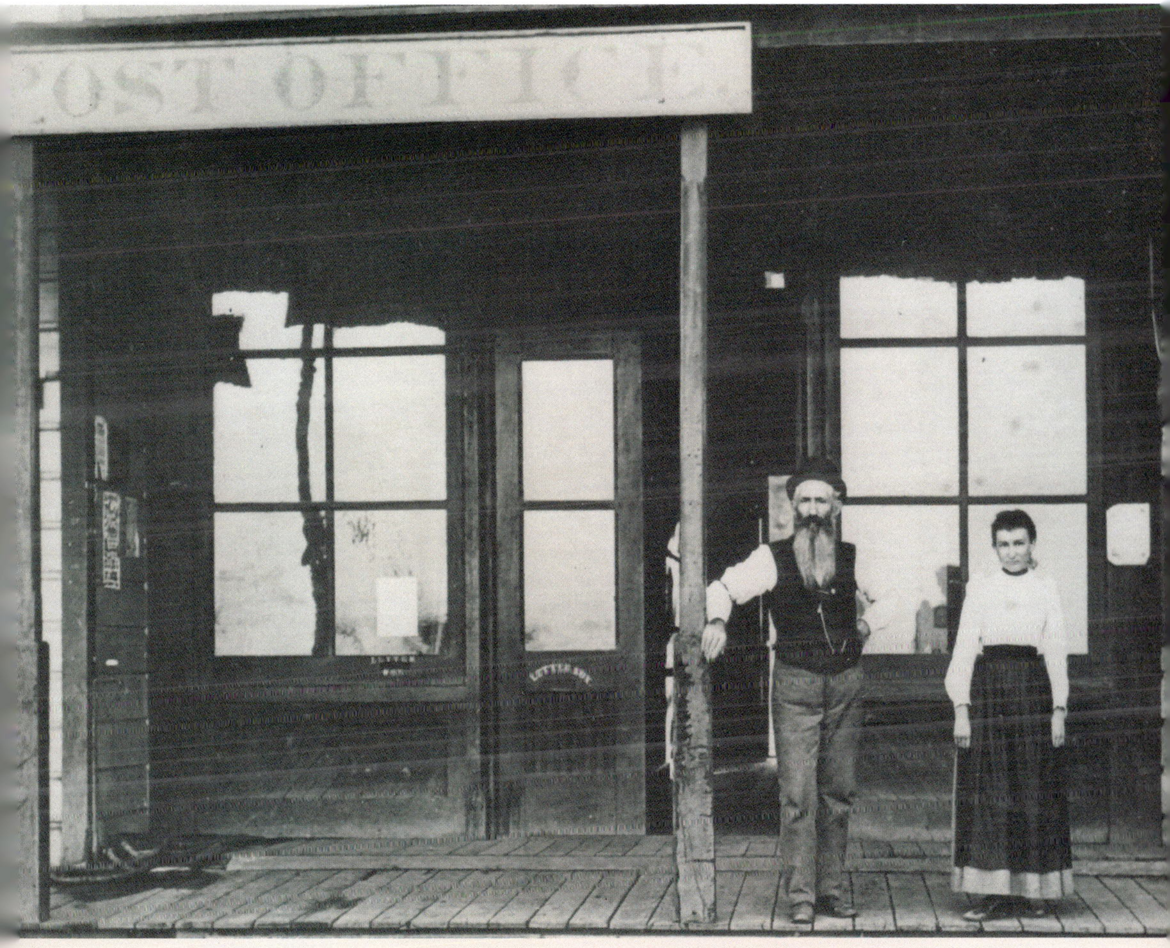

This is an 1890 photograph of San Pedro's first postmaster, Alberta Barton (right), standing in front of the post office on Front Street (presently Harbor Boulevard) between Fourth and Fifth Streets. Sidewalks are wooden planks, and the street had not been paved yet. The post office would be located on another site before being located on Beacon Street between Eighth and Ninth Streets.

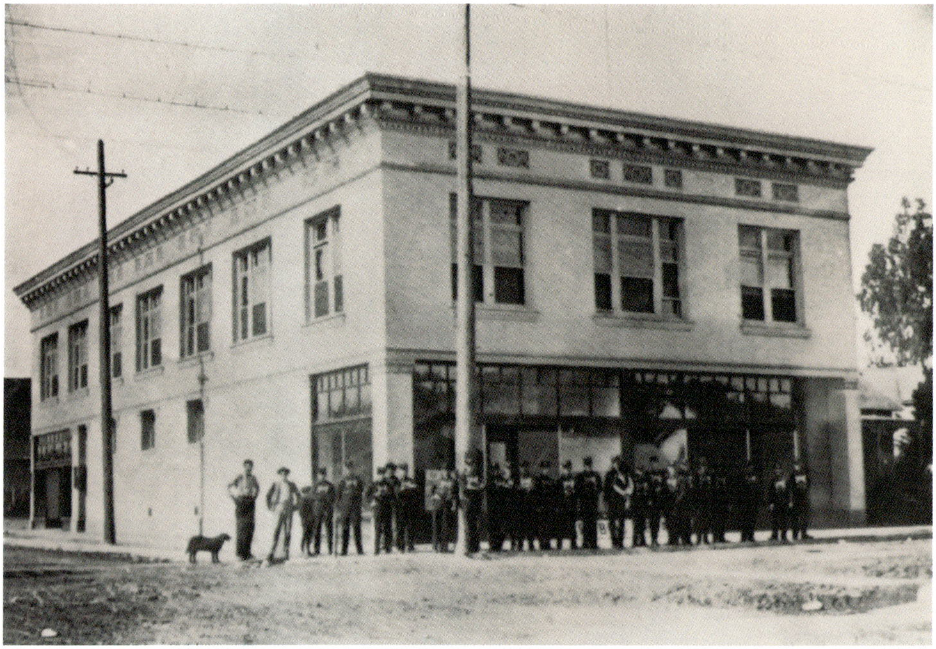

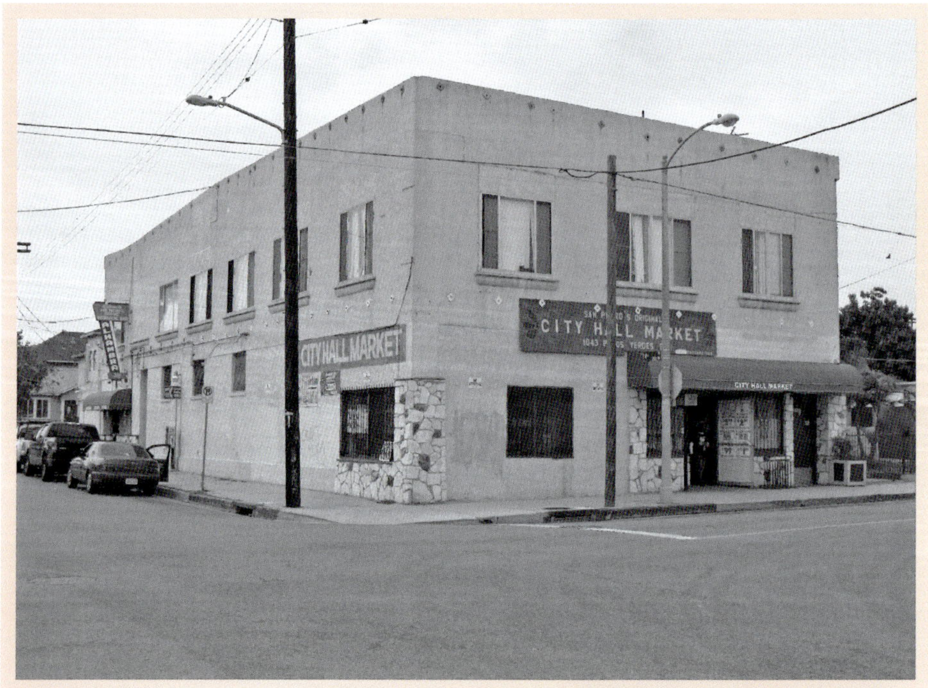

San Pedro's first city hall was located on the northwest corner of Eleventh and Palos Verdes Streets. Standing in front of the city hall in the 1905 photograph above is the San Pedro Volunteer Fire Department. The street appears to be unpaved. Today it is a neighborhood mini market appropriately named City Hall Market. Located in the rear of the market is the Alhambra Bar. Its sign claims that it is "San Pedro's Oldest Historic Bar . . . Since 1936."

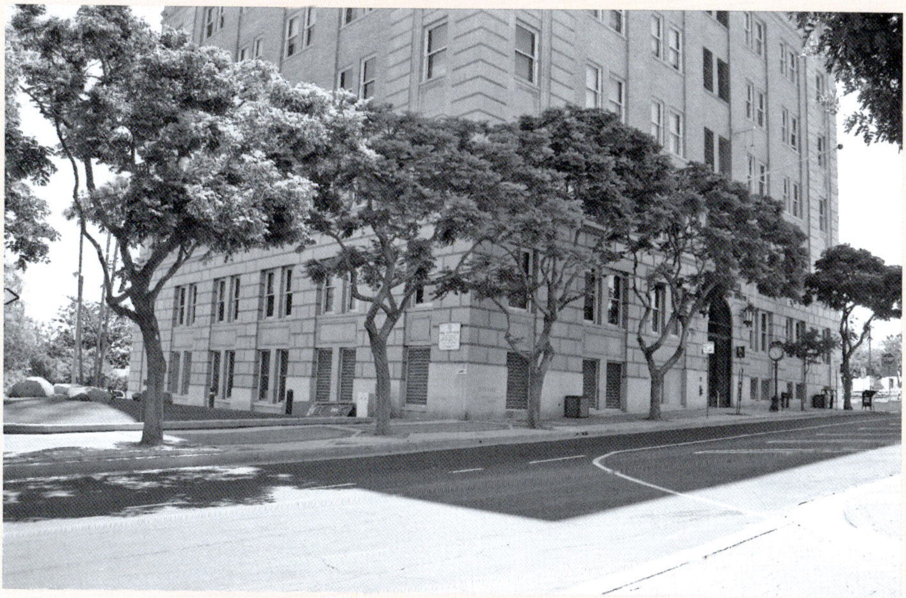

On February 22, 1928, the Native Sons of the Golden West laid the cornerstone of the municipal building. The photographer may have taken advantage of an upper floor of the Anderson building, which was directly across the street, to take the photograph below. The municipal building and its cornerstone are still in place today.

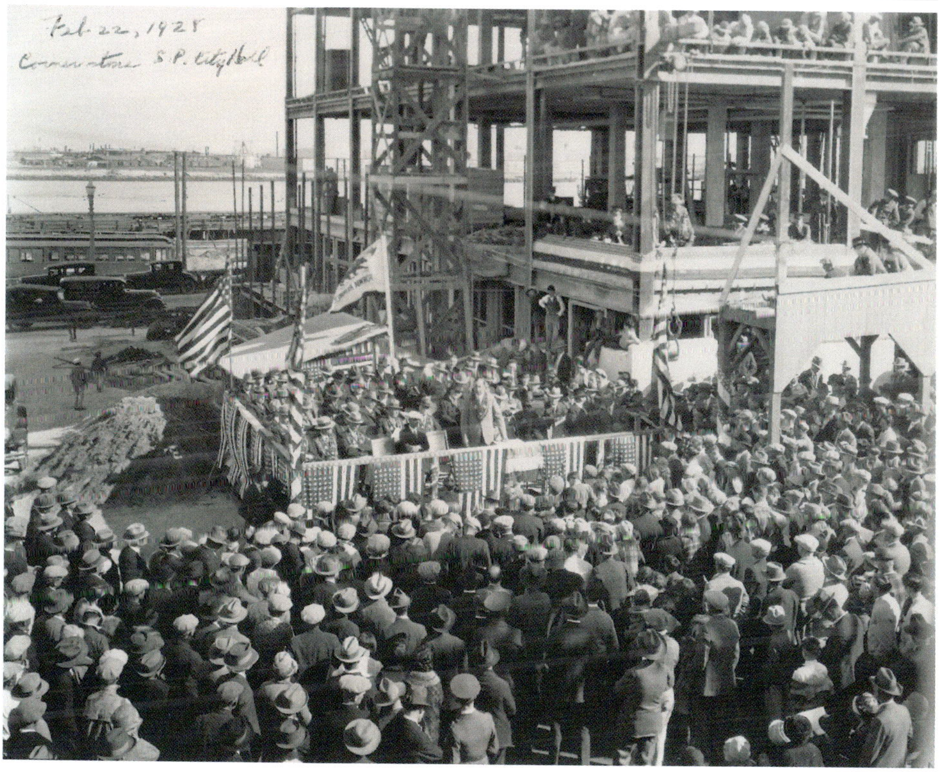

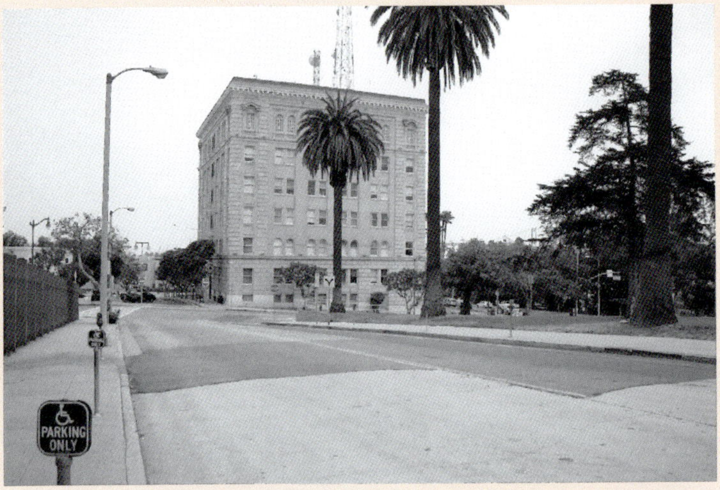

The municipal building, often referred to as San Pedro city hall, was dedicated in the fall of 1928. The building was never city hall, but it was built on the site of San Pedro's second city hall. The photograph below, taken on December 31, 1928, is looking south towards the building located on Seventh and Beacon Streets. There was a jail referred to as "Seventh Heaven" on the seventh floor. A section of jail still remains for tourists to view. Today the structure is still a functioning facility for the city of Los Angeles.

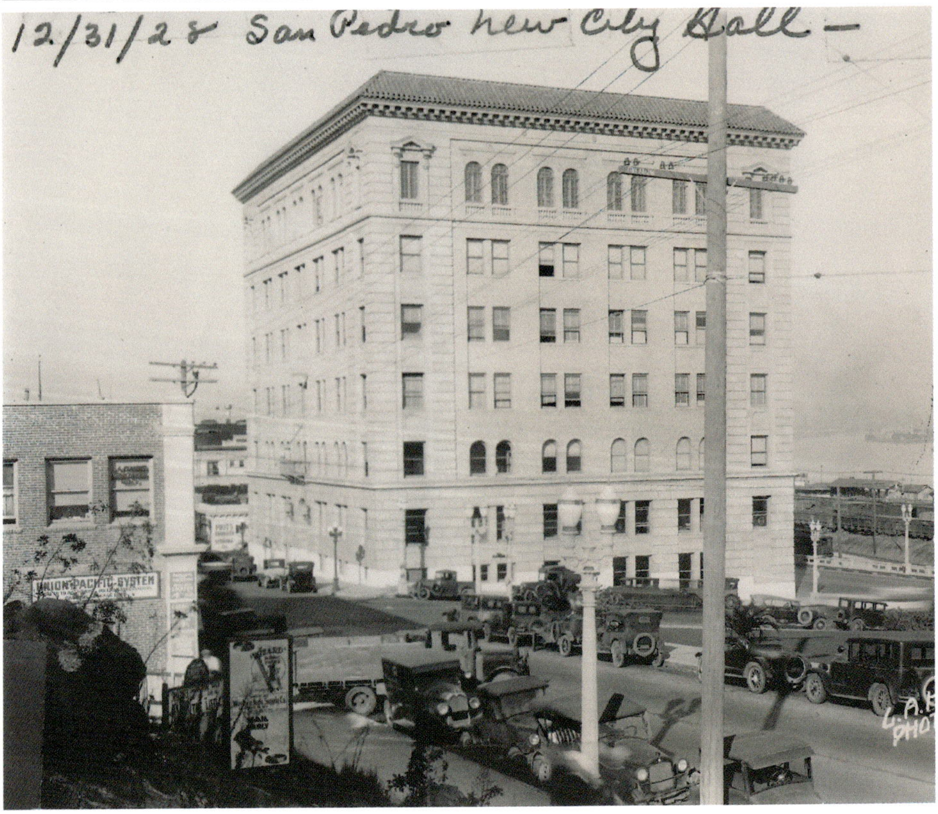

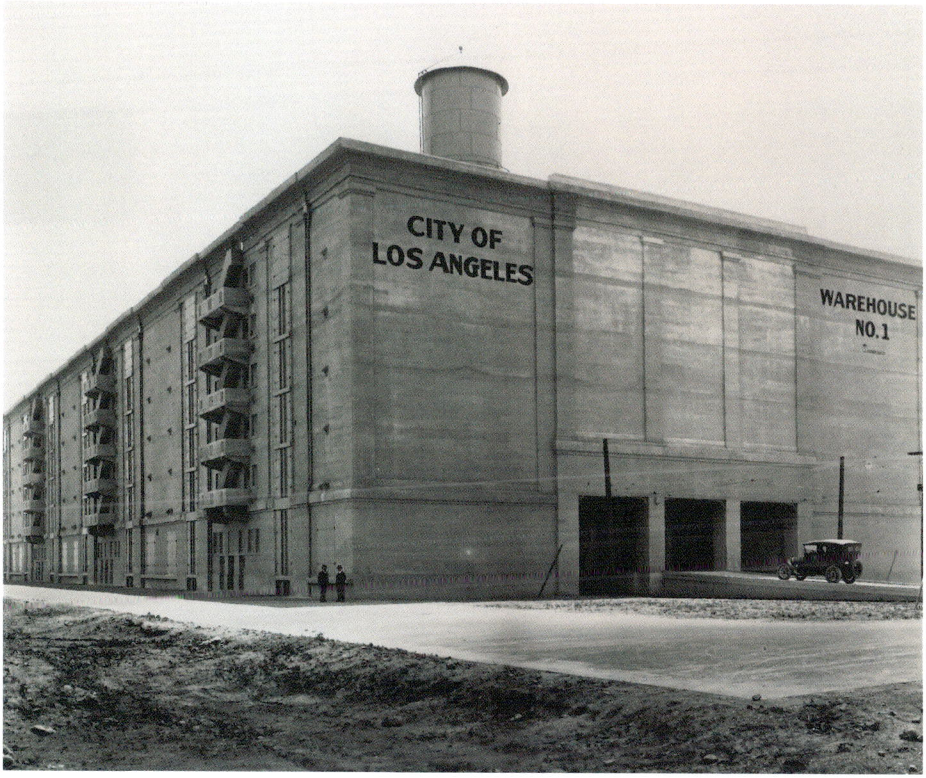

Los Angeles Warehouse No. 1 was completed in 1917. The 1916 photograph above shows two men posing at the north end of the structure. From 1917 to the early 1970s, this warehouse was an essential facility to the economic growth and success of the Port of Los Angeles. With the introduction of containerization of cargo in the early 1970s, such structures were no longer needed for warehousing. Warehouse No. 1 still stands at the entrance of San Pedro's deepwater channel and has been listed on the National Register of Historic Places since April 2000. The water tank on the top greets visitors to the harbor in many languages.

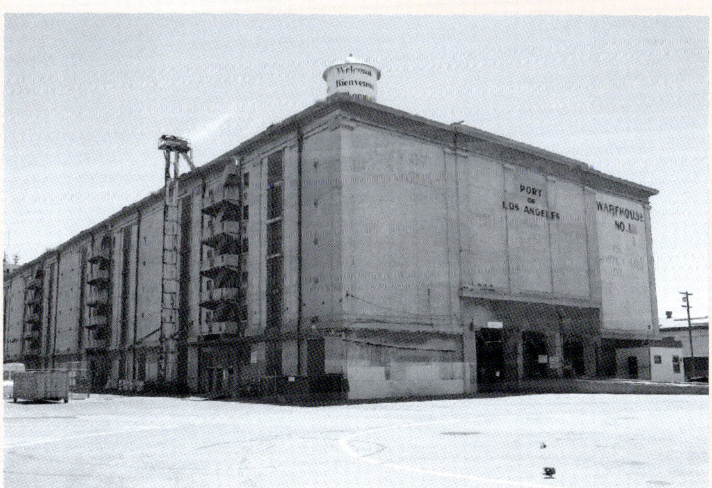

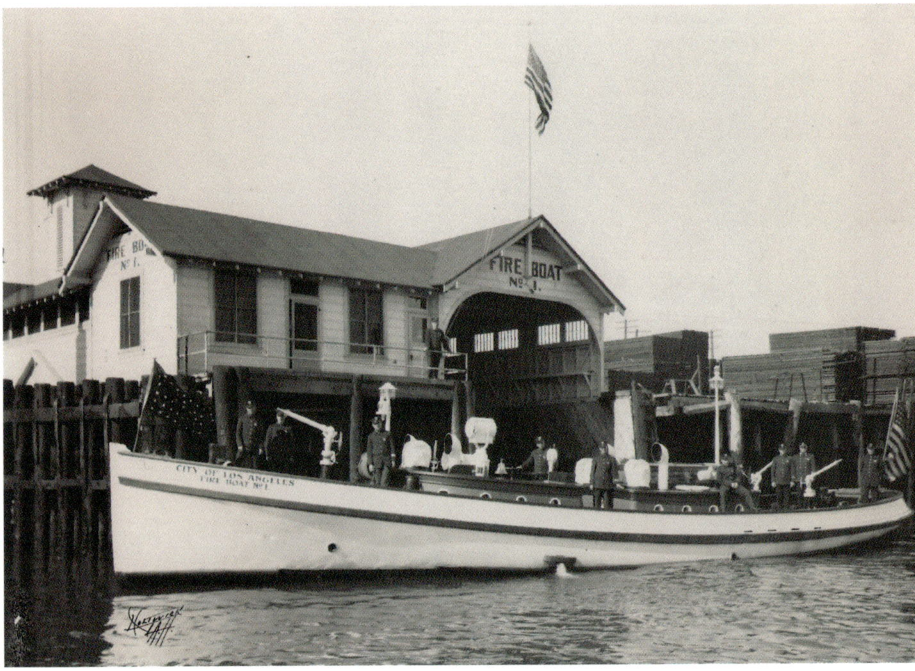

The Los Angeles Fire Department (LAFD) has had the responsibility of putting out harbor and ship fires for many years. LAFD's Fire Boat No.1 in the photograph above was commissioned in 1919 and moved to that station located at Fish Harbor on Terminal Island on May 2, 1927. The boat was later rechristened the *Archibald J. Eley* in 1965. A portion of the old station still stands and is a base for the Los Angeles Harbor Police Dive Team.

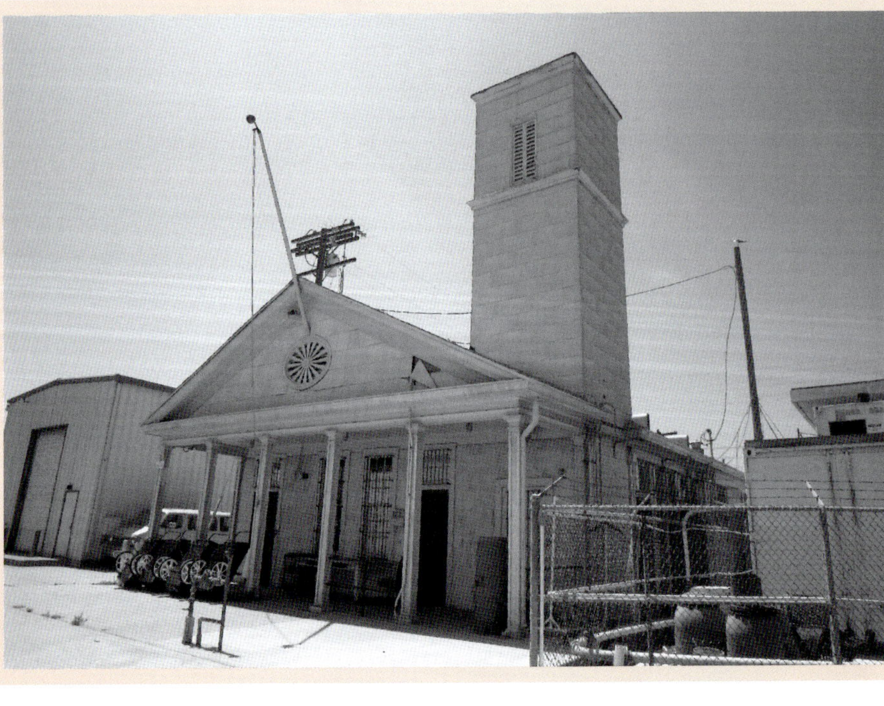

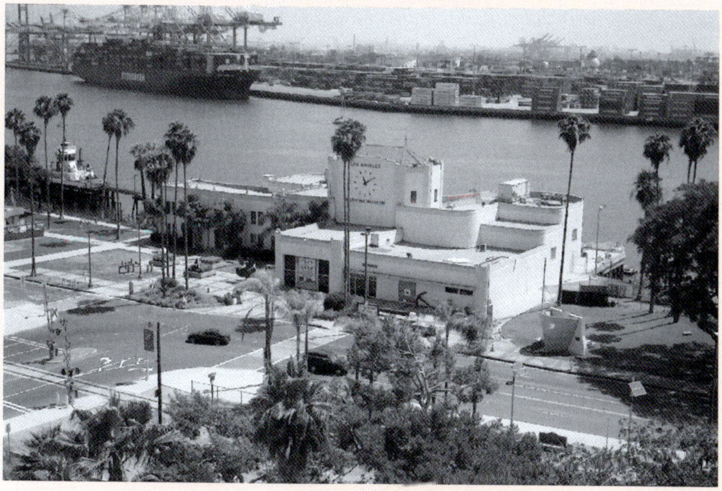

The 1941 photograph below shows the municipal ferry terminal located at the foot of Sixth Street across from Harbor Boulevard (Berth 84). Its sister terminal (right) was located on Terminal Island. The ferry *Islander* is midway through its five-minute trip to the mainland terminal. Fare for this service was 5¢ per person and 25¢ per automobile. In the foreground are two northbound Pacific Electric streetcars. Naval ships are docked at Terminal Island. That area is now a ship container yard. The ferry service ran from 1941 until the Vincent Thomas Bridge opened in 1963. The *Islander* made about 450,000 round-trips across the main channel during its time of service. Since 1980, this art deco building has housed the Los Angeles Maritime Museum. It is listed on the National Register of Historic Places.

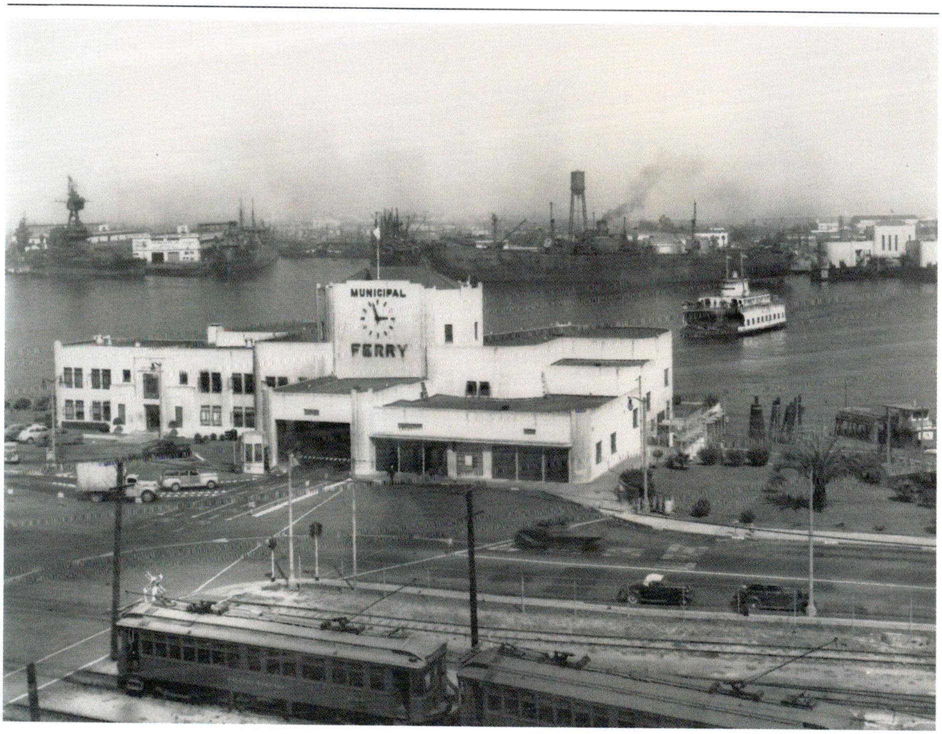

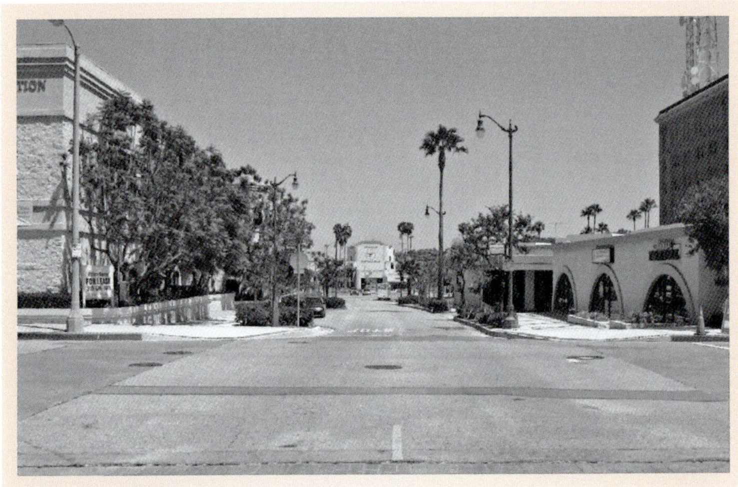

Below is an early 1960s photograph of Sixth Street looking east across Palos Verdes Street that shows a number of bars and some hotels in this area of San Pedro. On the south side (right) are the Back Bay Hotel, Club Del Rio, the Alaska Inn, and the Skipper Inn. In the left background, a corner of the Alexander Hotel is visible. The iconic municipal ferry terminal is in the center background and was still providing ferry service when this photograph was taken. All buildings, except the municipal ferry terminal, in the old photograph were demolished as part of the Beacon Street redevelopment project in the early 1970s.

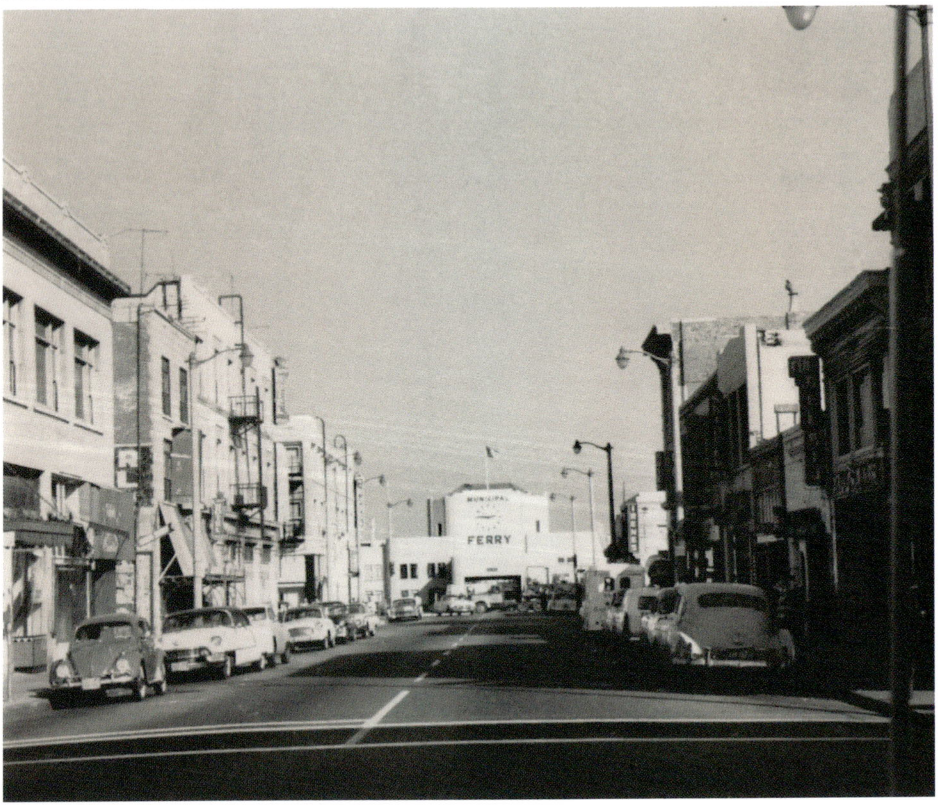

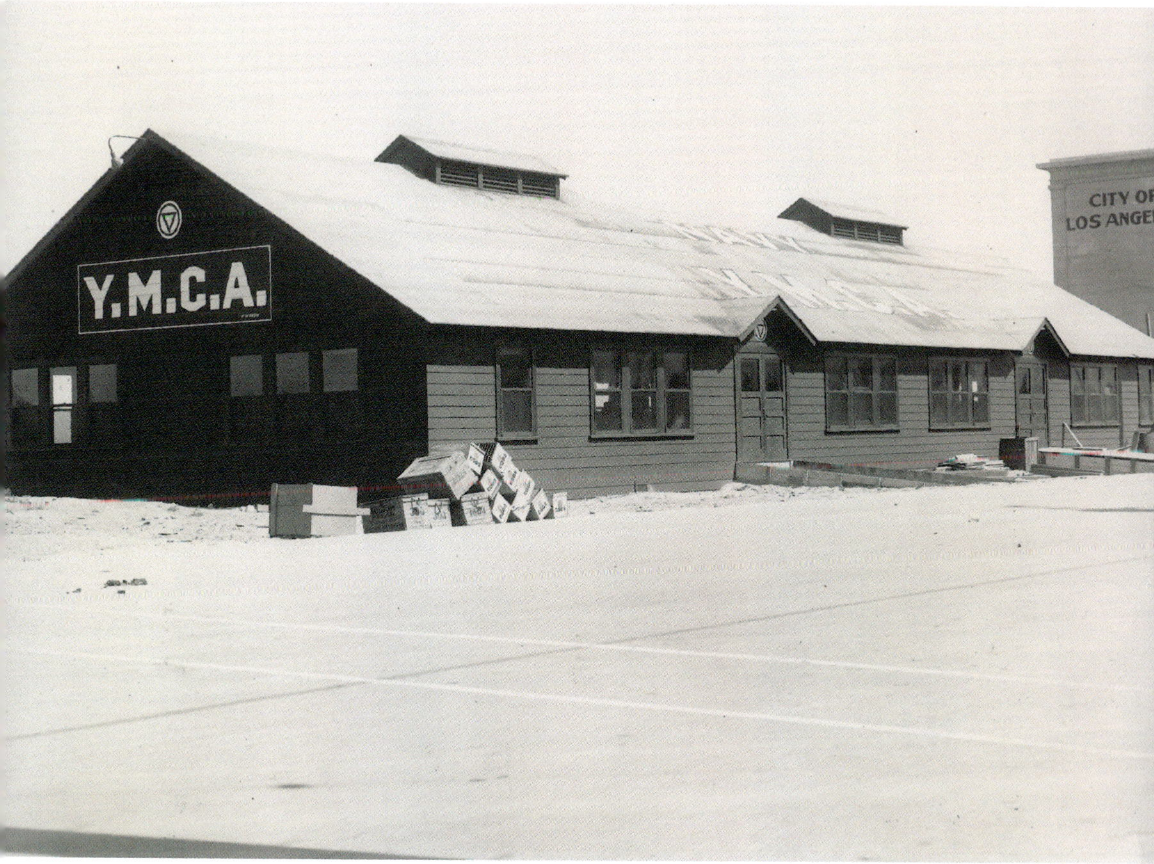

On September 8, 1917, the photograph above was taken of the Navy YMCA located just north of Los Angeles Warehouse No. 1. Construction on the warehouse was completed the same year. The army/navy YMCA, a larger and less spartan facility, was later constructed in 1926 on Beacon Street between Ninth and Tenth Streets. The property is now the location for petroleum product storage tanks.

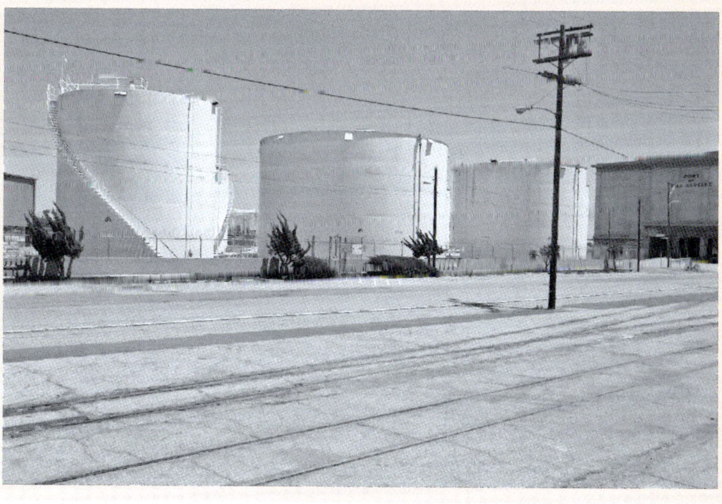

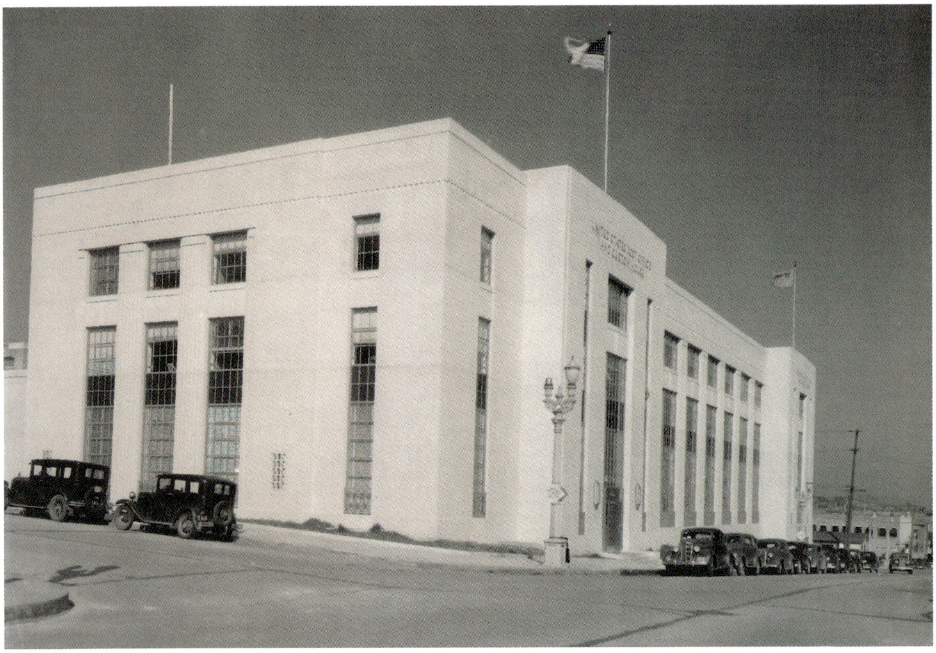

The San Pedro post office and U.S. Customs House is an excellent example of a Public Works Administration project. It was completed in 1936 on the west side of South Beacon Street between West Eighth and Ninth Streets. The building's streamline modern (a type of art deco in the 1930s) exterior, marble interior, and Works Progress Administration mural in the lobby has made this building a San Pedro landmark. It is on the National Register of Historic Places. The post office continues to serve the San Pedro community, but the U.S. Customs House is no longer at that location. The sign on the left side of the building is advertising space available for lease. Private businesses now have offices in the building.

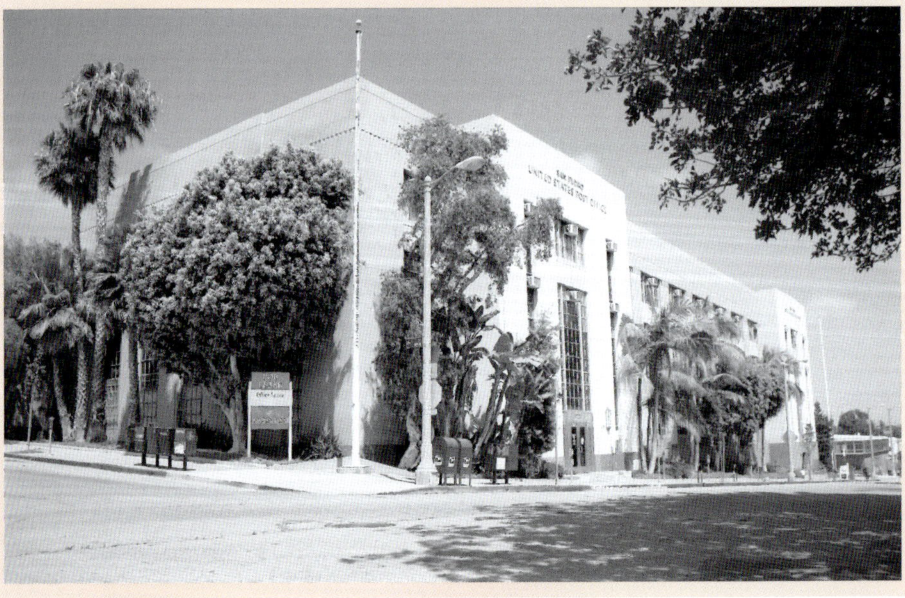

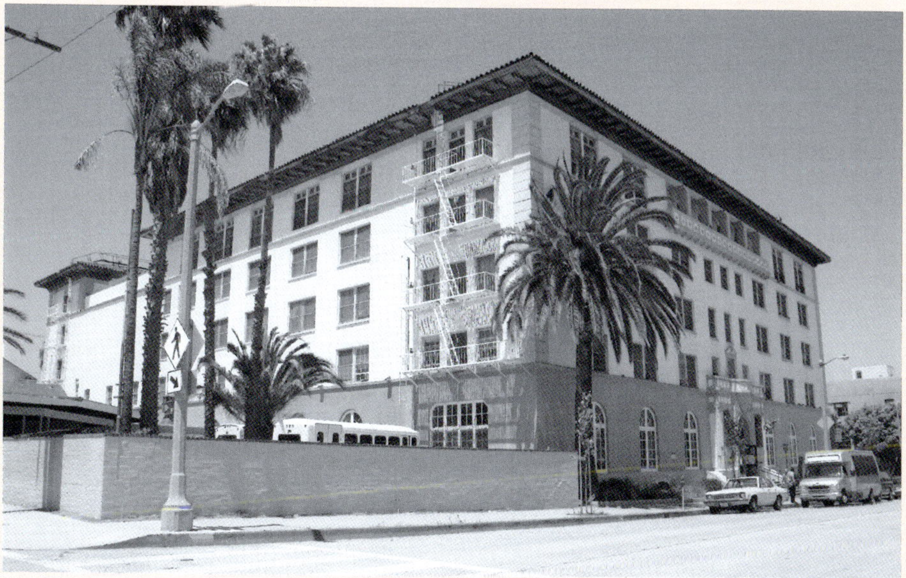

The army/navy YMCA located on the west side of Beacon Street between Ninth and Tenth Streets was completed in 1926. Now named Harbor View House, it is an agency of the city of Los Angeles.

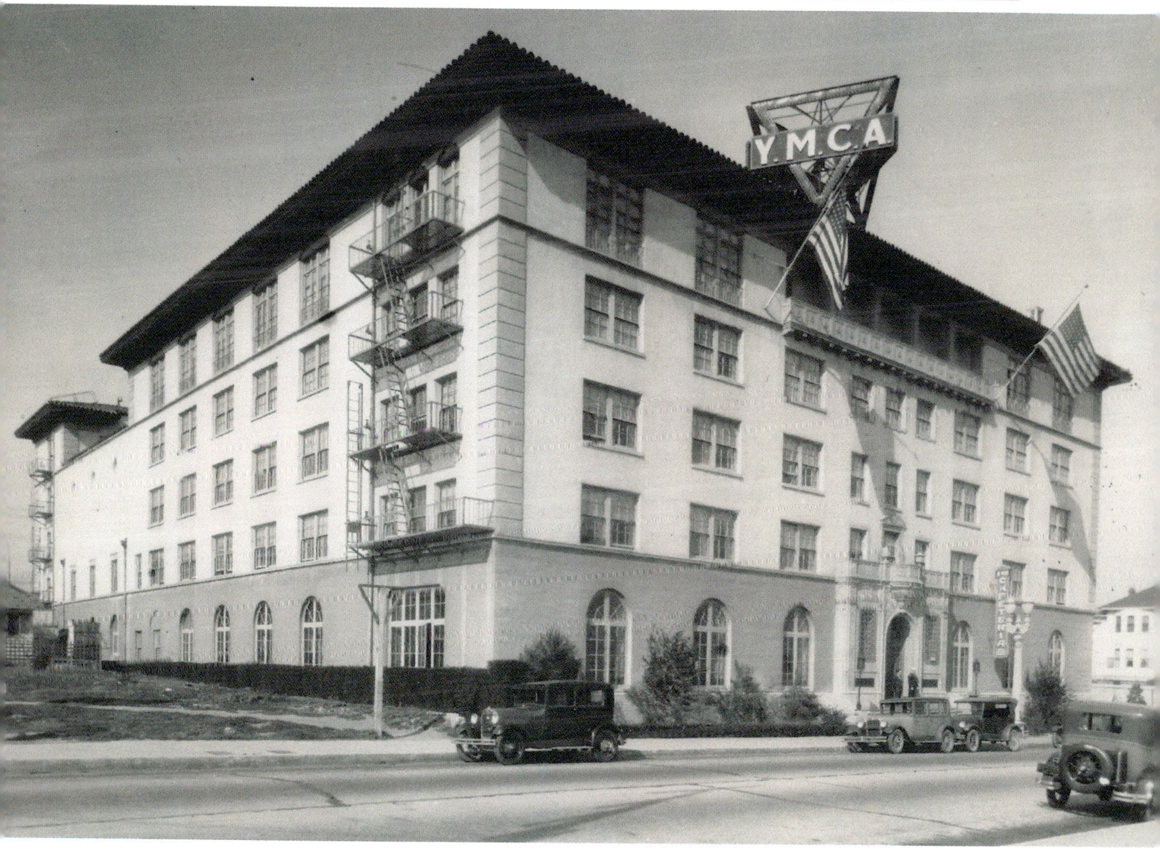

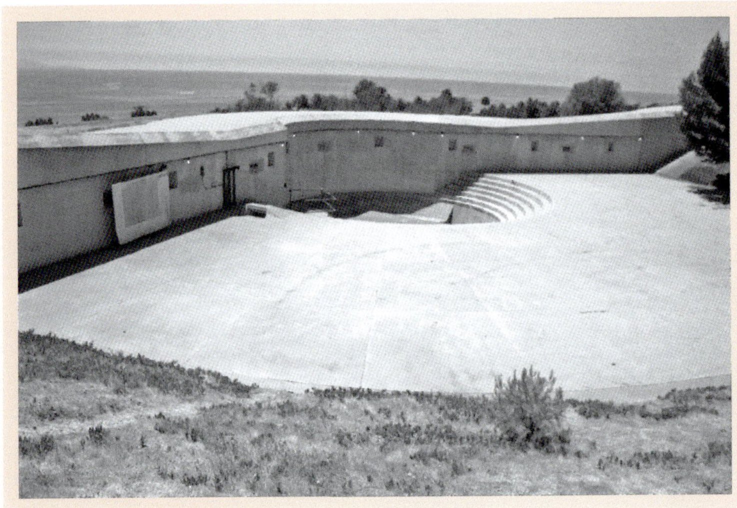

Training sessions for soldiers on how to safely operate the 14-inch guns of Battery Osgood-Farley, located at the Upper Reservation of Fort MacArthur, were very important. The Osgood gun pictured in the 1925 photograph below was constructed during the years 1916 through 1919. The adjacent Farley gun was constructed during the same period. The gun is mounted on what is called a disappearing carriage—the gun was raised above the wall and it retracted (disappeared) behind the wall when fired. It was capable of firing a 1,560-pound projectile 14 miles. In 1944, the guns of Battery Osgood-Farley were declared surplus and cut up for scrap after 1946. Only the battery fortifications of the gun placements remain. The Osgood gun placement is the only one where the counterweight hole has not been filled in.

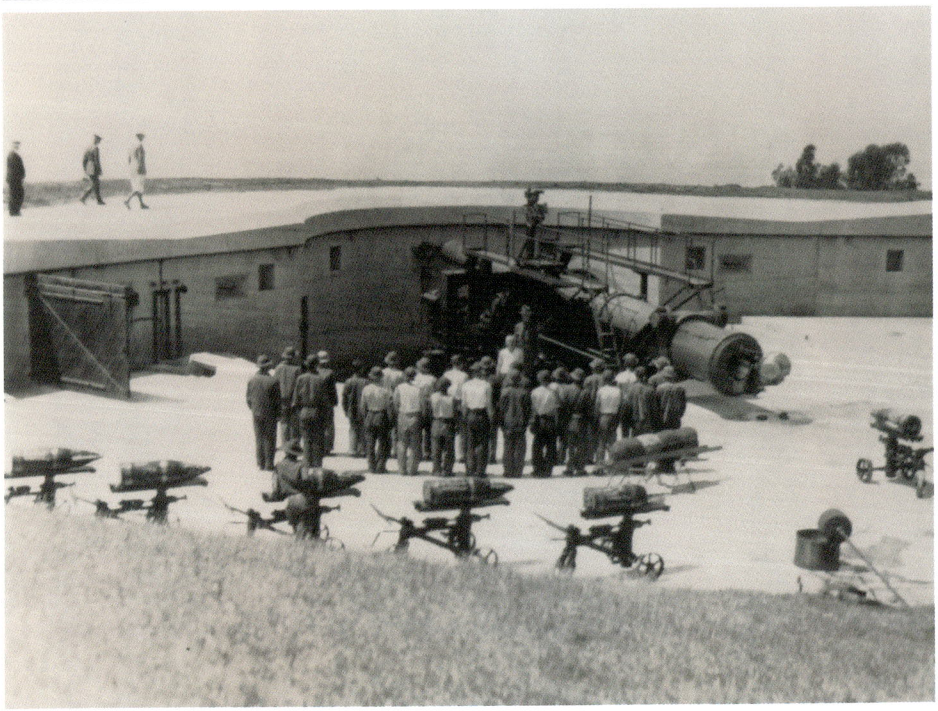

CHAPTER 4

Businesses and Other Buildings

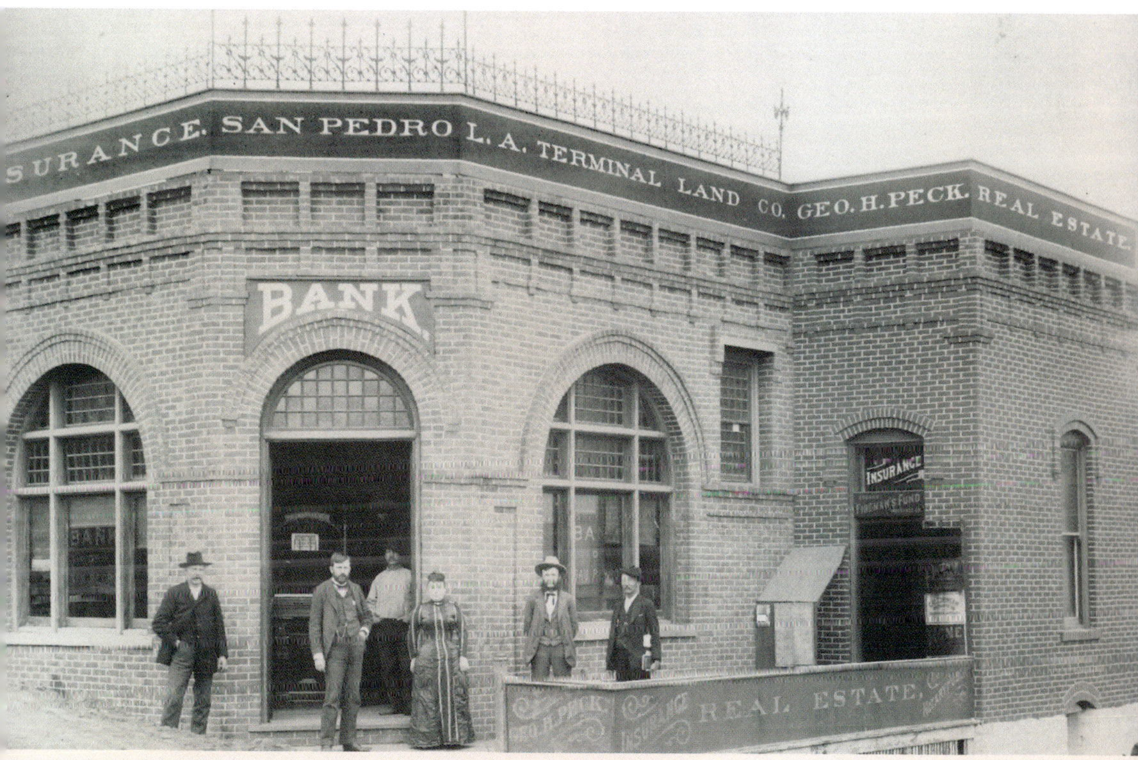

Commerce is vital to the growth and development of communities and cities. This 1913 photograph is of the business headquarters of George H. Peck, one of San Pedro's foremost movers and shakers. He provided insurance, real estate, and banking services. The bank is the Bank of San Pedro. The building was located on Beacon Street between Sixth and Seventh Streets. Though not identified, the man standing in front of bank's door could be Peck.

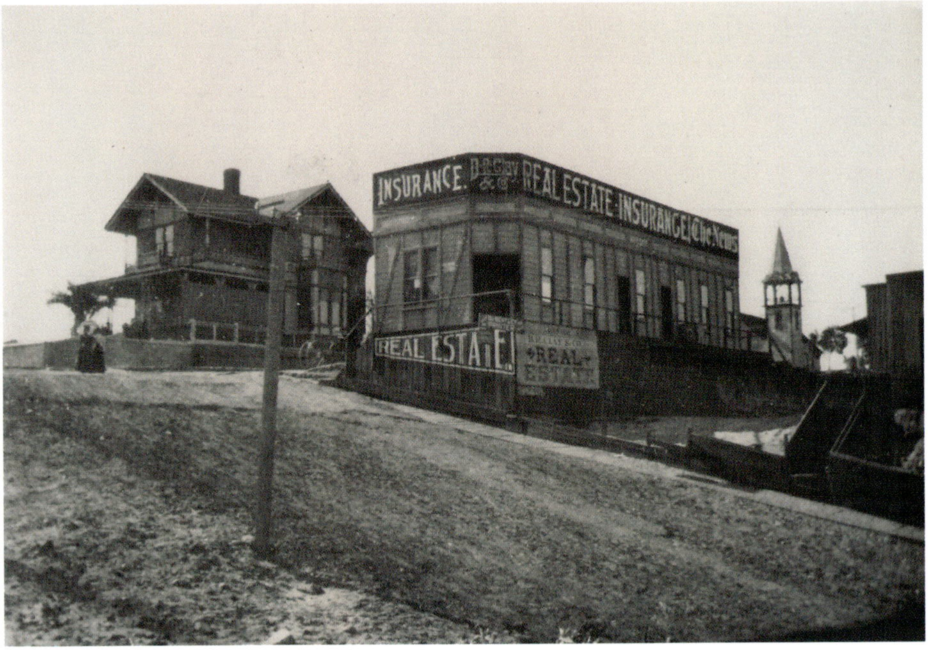

The Dodson house was built in 1882 as a wedding present by the Sepulveda family for their daughter Rudecinda, who married James H. Dodson. The *c.* 1888 photograph above shows the house (left) in its original location at Seventh and Beacon Streets. Across the street was the D. R. Clay and Company real estate office. The house has been moved twice; it is now located on West Thirteenth Street and has been owned by the Reed family as a private residence since 1954. The elevation of Seventh and Beacon Streets has been significantly lowered. The present-day photograph shows the general location where the two historical structures were located. In the area where the Dodson house and D. R. Clay Real Estate were located are now a parking lot, a pediatric clinic, and nearby, the San Pedro post office.

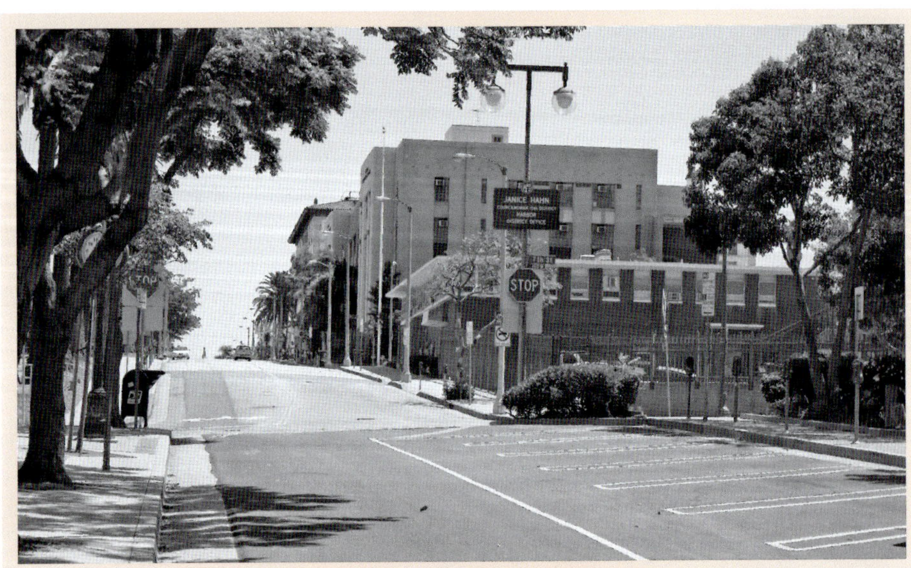

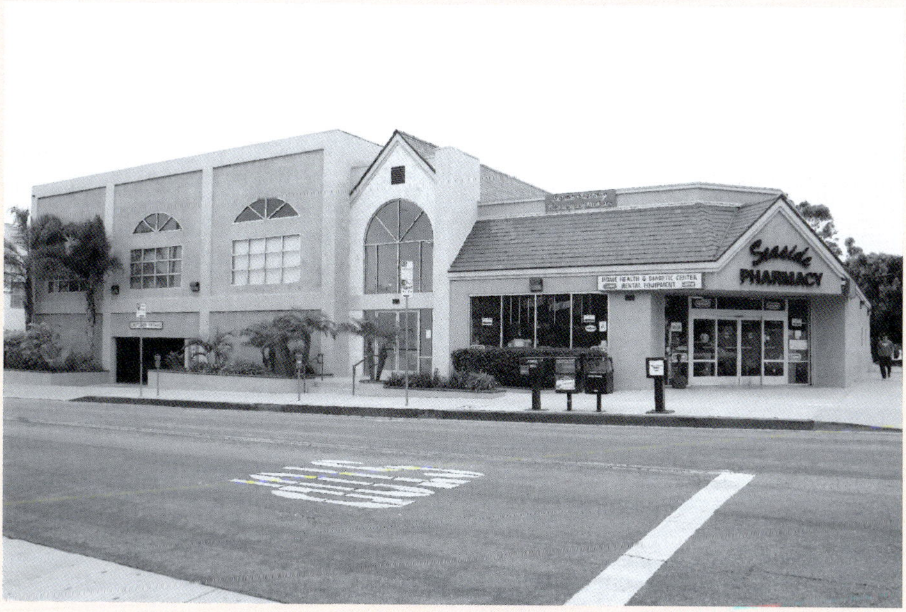

San Pedro's oldest pharmacy and business is Seaside Pharmacy. It was founded in 1889, on the southwest corner of Sixth and Beacon Streets (below). The pharmacy later moved to the corner of Fifth and Front Streets—now Harbor Boulevard. Most of the block where the pharmacy was first located was demolished to make room for the Anderson building. A Mexican restaurant presently occupies the property. The present-day photograph above shows Seaside Pharmacy at its fourth location, which opened in 1999 on Seventh and Grand Streets. (Vintage photograph courtesy of Seaside Pharmacy.)

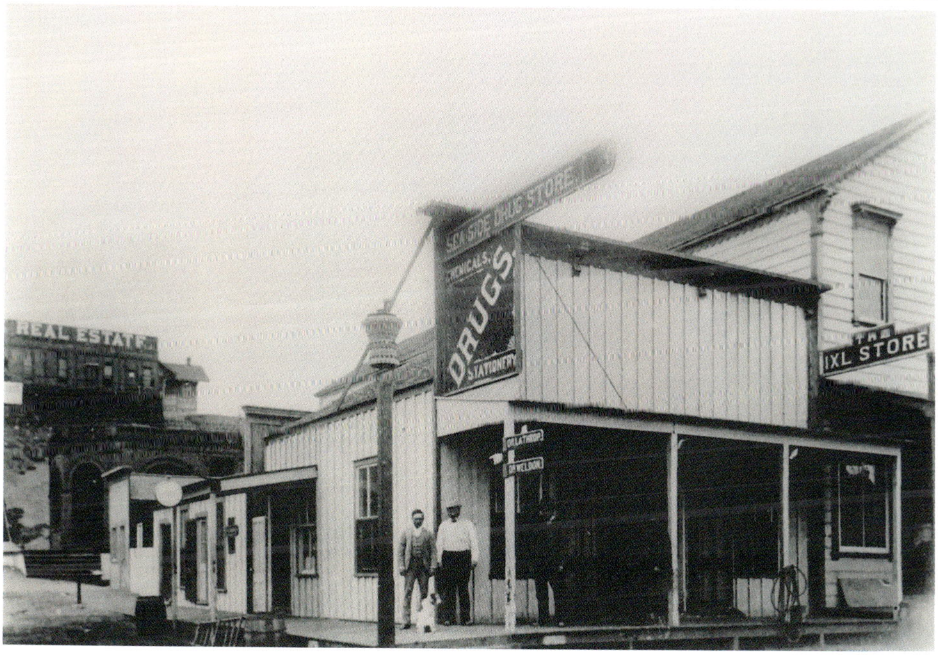

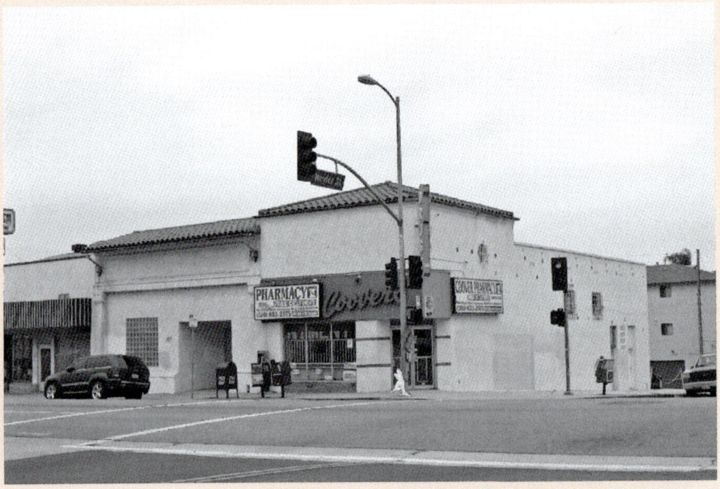

Coover's Drugs has been in business since 1922 at the 800 block of West Ninth Street. In the *c.* 1940 photograph below, Coover's was next to "Wrangler's 9th & Meyler Market." The drugstore has since expanded into what was once Wrangler's Market and now goes by the name Coover's Pharmacy. Bicycles dropped off at the curb in the 1940s photograph might indicate that kids were inside Coover's buying a treat at the soda fountain.

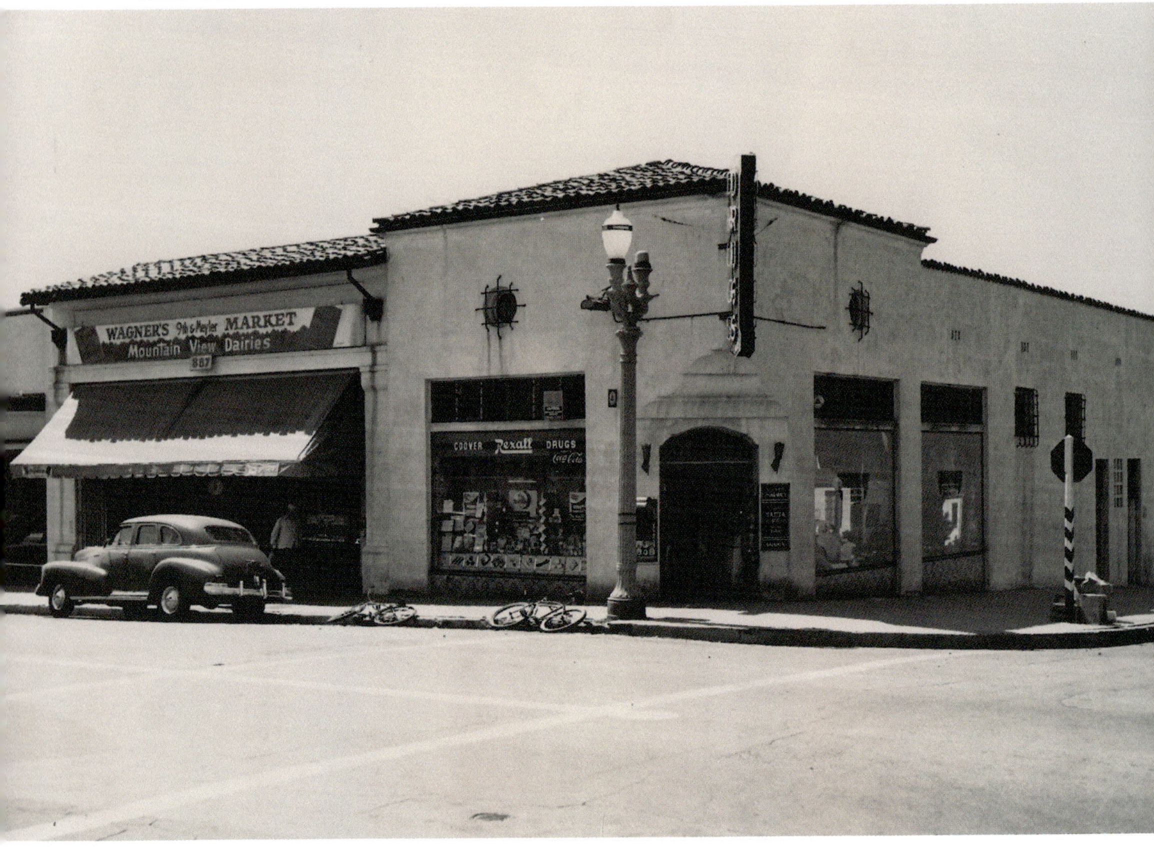

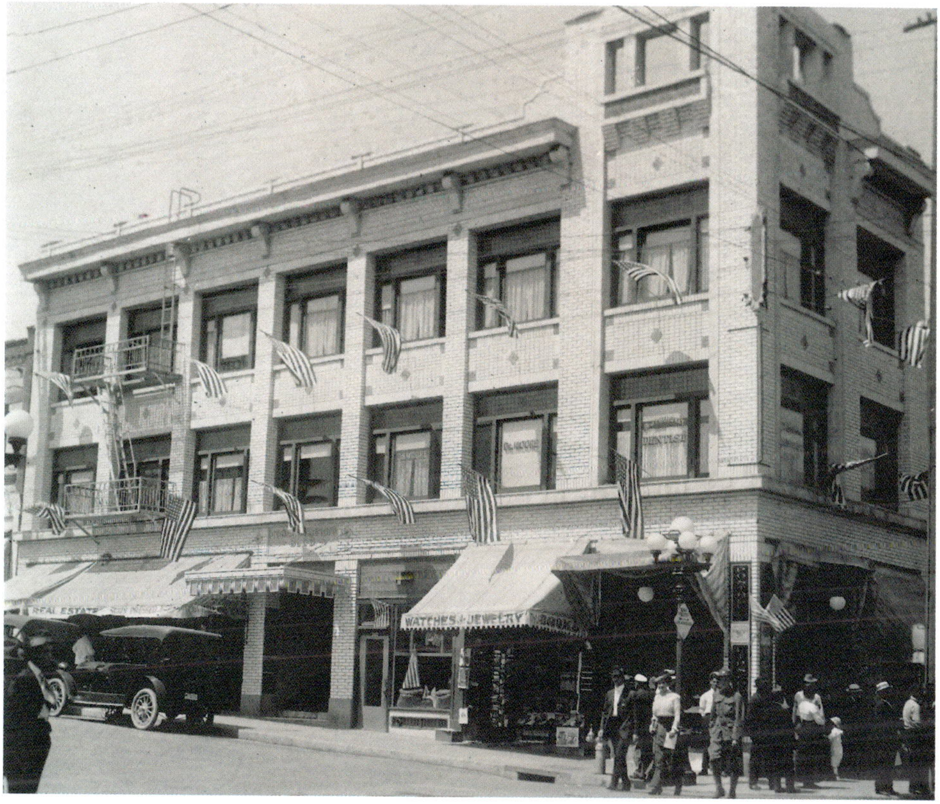

The N. O. Anderson building was located on the southwest corner of the intersection of Sixth and Beacon Streets. The offices of two physicians and a dentist were on the second floor when the above photograph was taken around 1919. The number of American flags on the building would suggest this photograph was taken on or near a patriotic holiday. At the building's ground level there was a book and jewelry store, a place where a man could get his suit pressed, and a real estate office. The corner is now the site of the Green Onion Mexican Restaurant.

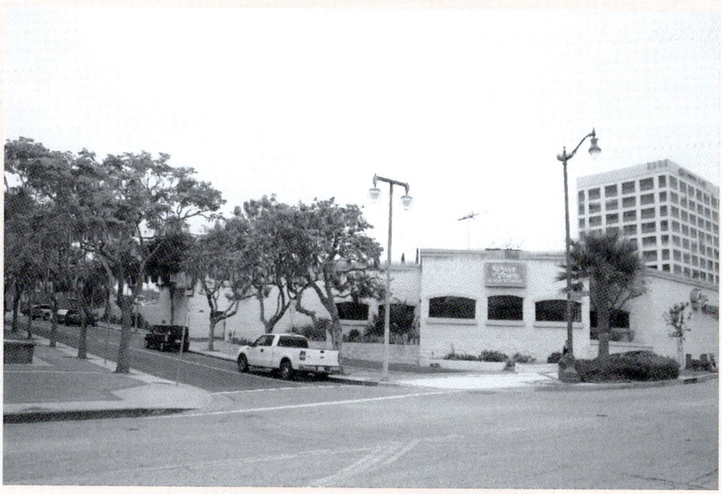

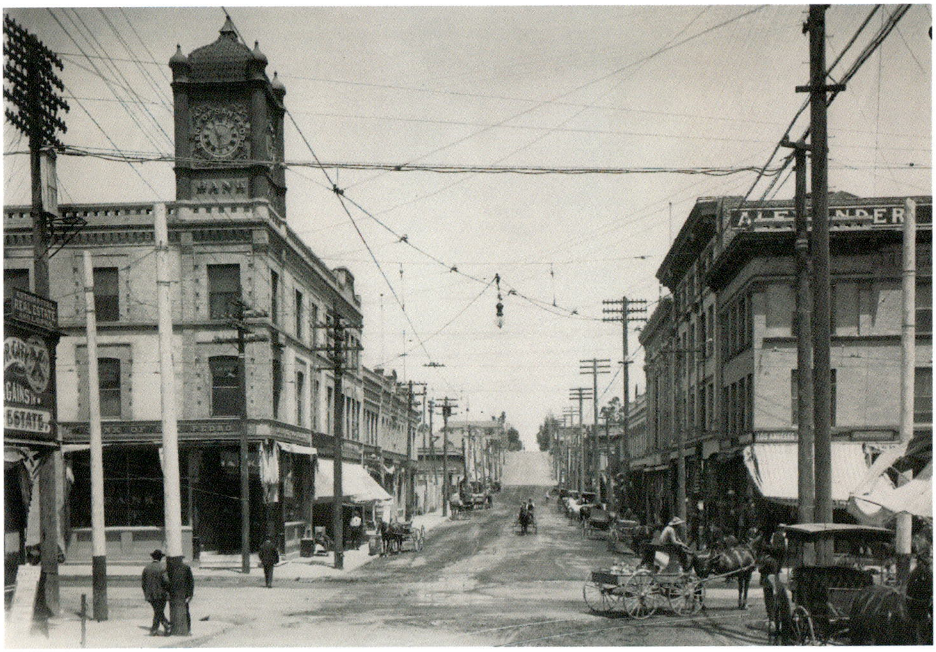

The *c.* 1910 photograph above could be considered an iconic image of San Pedro of the 1900s. Taken on Beacon Street facing north, the west side of the Alexander Hotel is on the right, and a branch of the Bank of San Pedro is on the left. Headquarters for the Bank of San Pedro was on Seventh and Mesa Streets. Horse-drawn carriages were still the major mode of transportation during that time, but the presence of wires hanging over the center of the streets indicates electric streetcars had been introduced to San Pedro. Now on the site where the Bank of San Pedro stood is an office building that was once used by American President Lines. Where the Alexander Hotel once stood is the Sunrise Hotel.

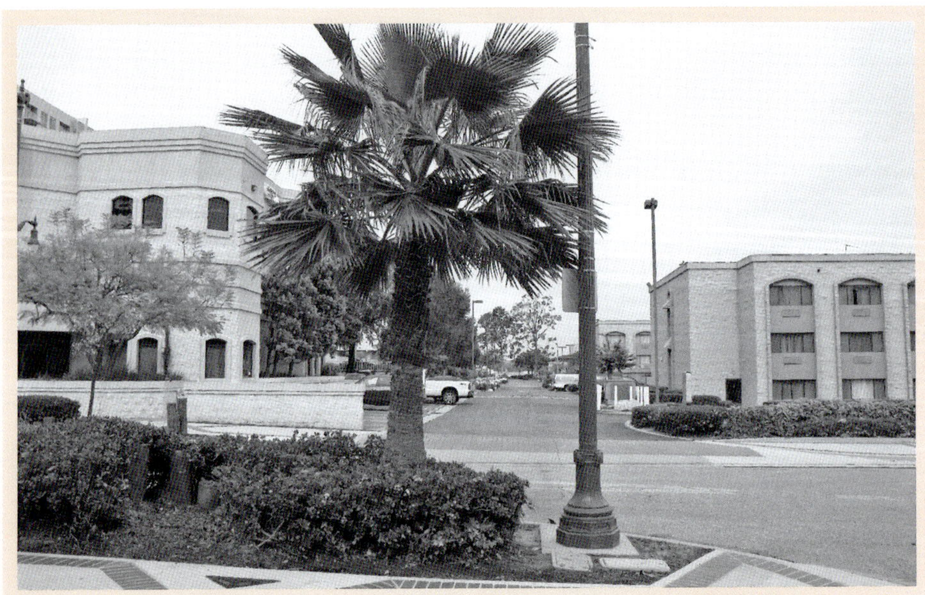

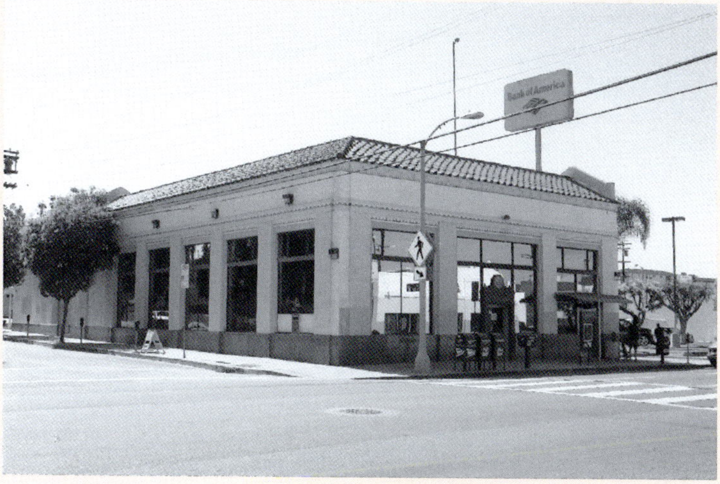

This branch of the Bank of America, in the *c.* 1930 photograph below, could possibly be the oldest operating bank in San Pedro. Located on the northwest corner of Tenth Street and South Pacific Avenue, this branch still provides banking services to the community. A new sign and automated teller machines are a couple of obvious changes. The surrounding property was bought and buildings demolished to provide a large parking lot for today's customers.

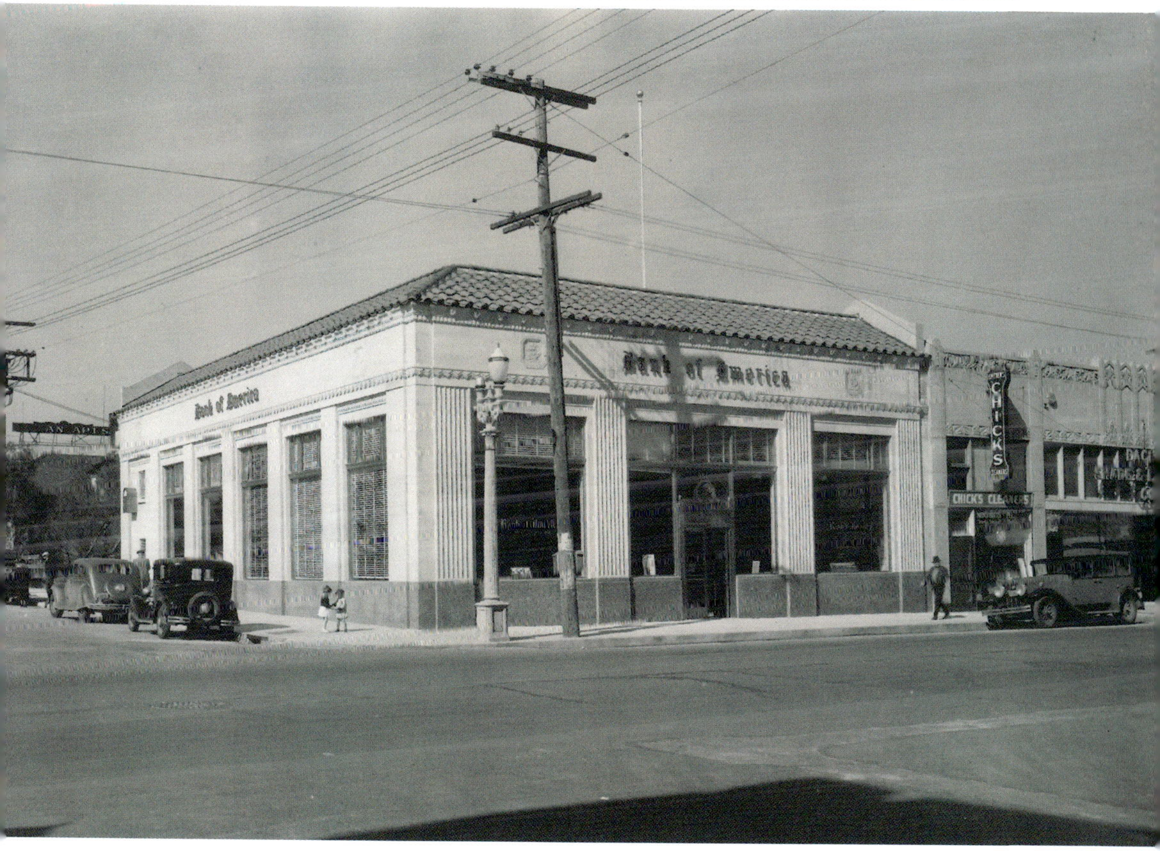

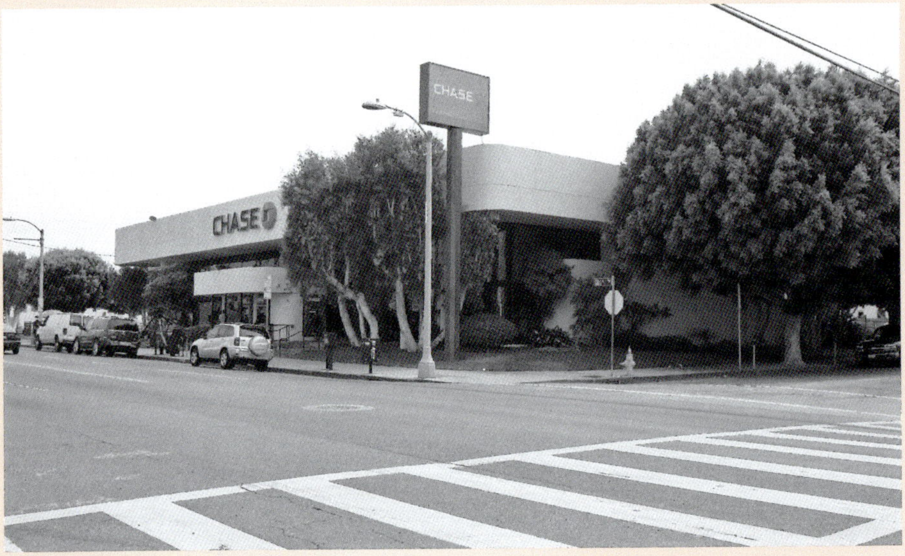

California Bank, situated on the southwest corner of Tenth Street and Pacific Avenue, is pictured in the late 1920s photograph below. Many years later a major renovation was done to the building. Prior to becoming a branch of Chase Bank, the building was home to Washington Mutual.

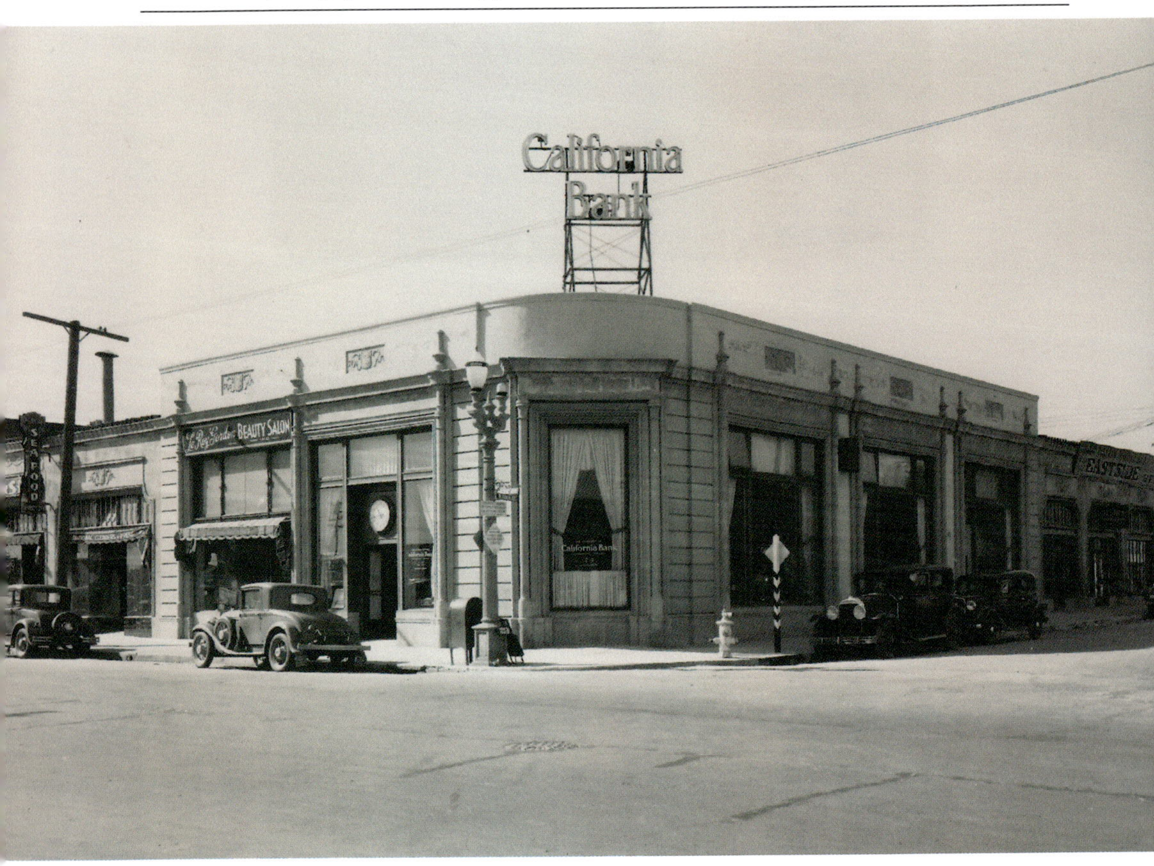

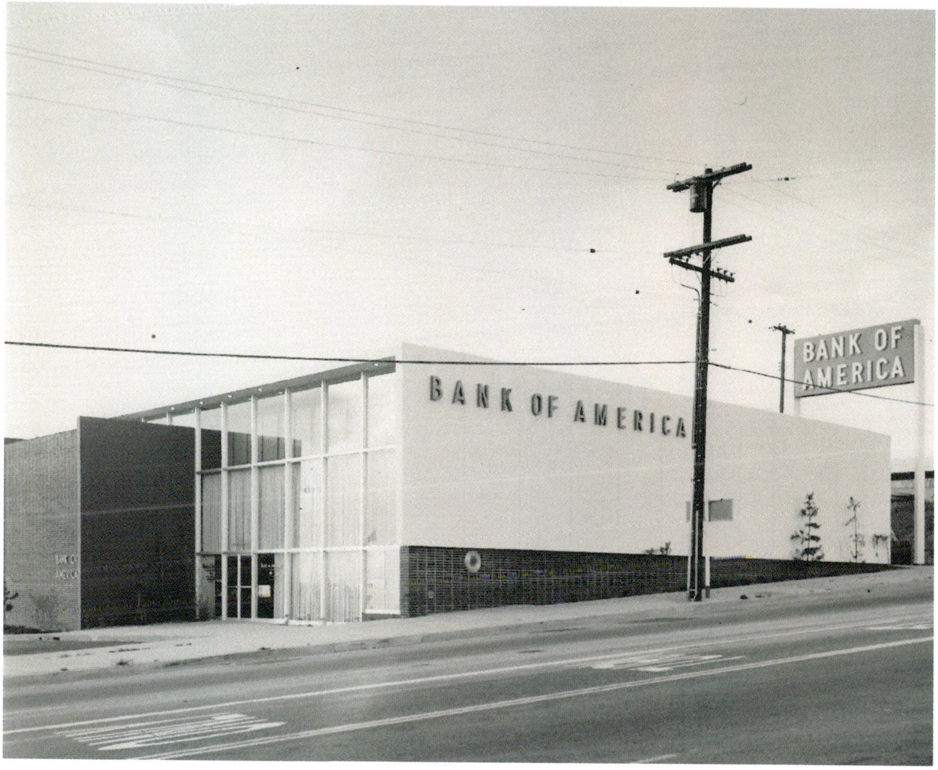

The third branch of Bank of America built in San Pedro opened in early 1960 on the northwest corner of Twenty-fifth Street and Western Avenue. This branch continues to provide banking services for the community. The present-day photograph below shows that except for signs and ATMs, very little has been done to change the exterior of the structure.

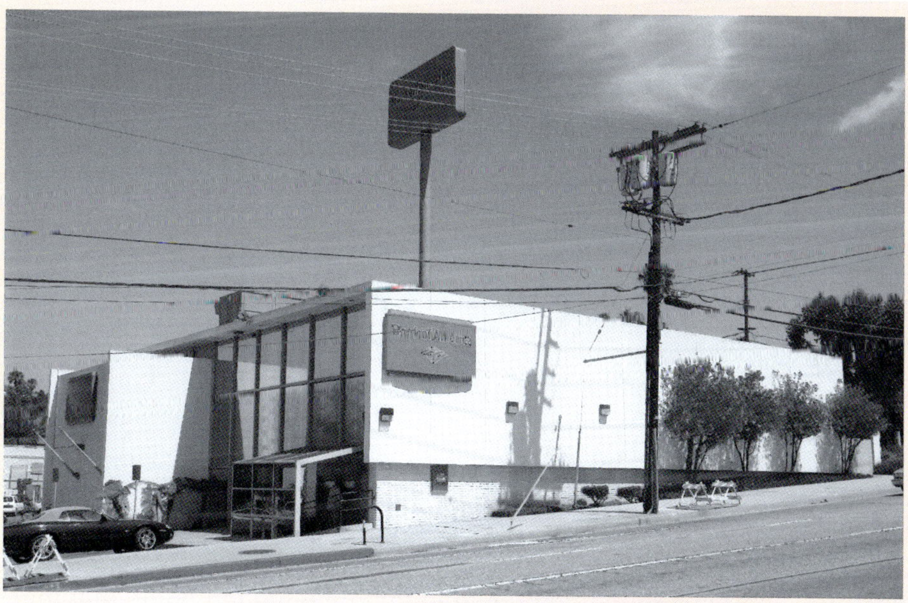

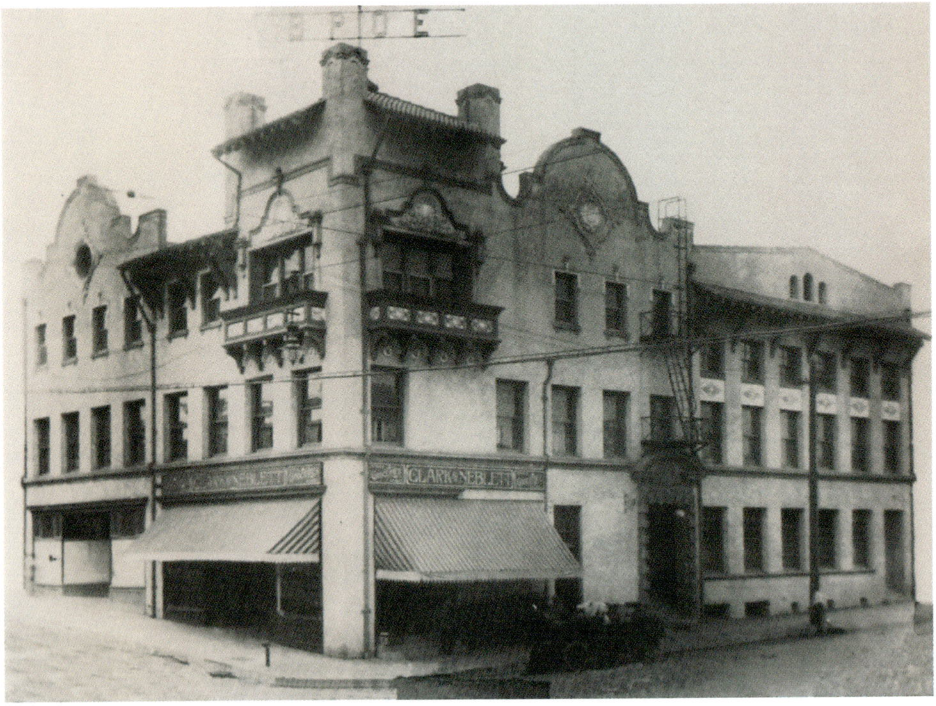

The San Pedro Elks Lodge No. 966 was located on the southwest corner of Seventh and Palos Verdes Streets after moving from the Masonic Hall on Beacon Street. It was dedicated on May 19, 1911. The lodge's ornate features were removed when it was later renovated. The building has since been demolished, and the site is now a parking lot for City of Los Angeles employees. The Elks built a larger facility on Cumbre Drive in San Pedro that was dedicated in the early 1960s.

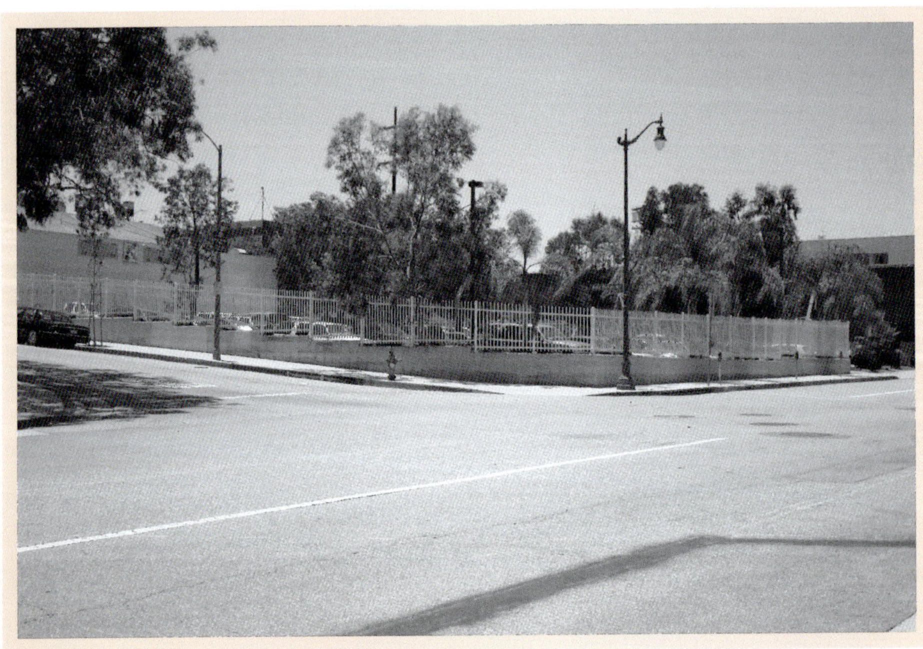

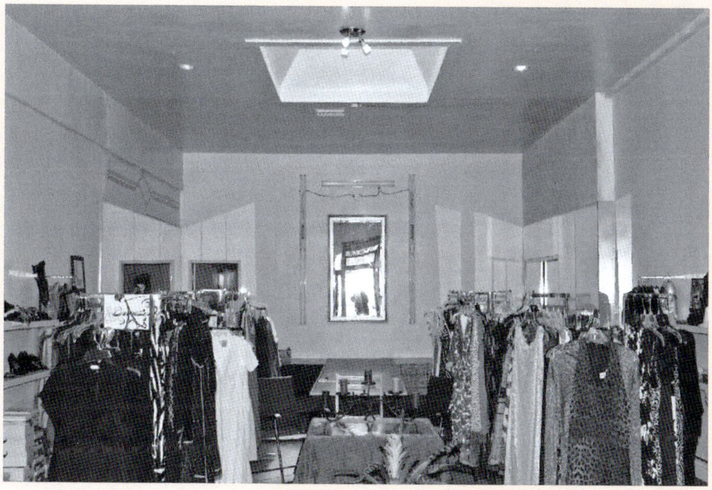

Sunset Photo was instrumental in chronicling the history of San Pedro and the development of the harbor area on film from the 1900s to the late 1920s. Sunset Photo Supply was located at 319 West Sixth Street when the *c.* 1921 photograph below was taken. A sign in the back of the shop reads, "Films left at 9 a.m. will be finished by 5. Films left after 9 a.m. will be finished at 5 the following day." Dramatique—Women's Specialty Clothing, which now occupies that space, opened in April 2010. The skylight is still a prominent feature in the store.

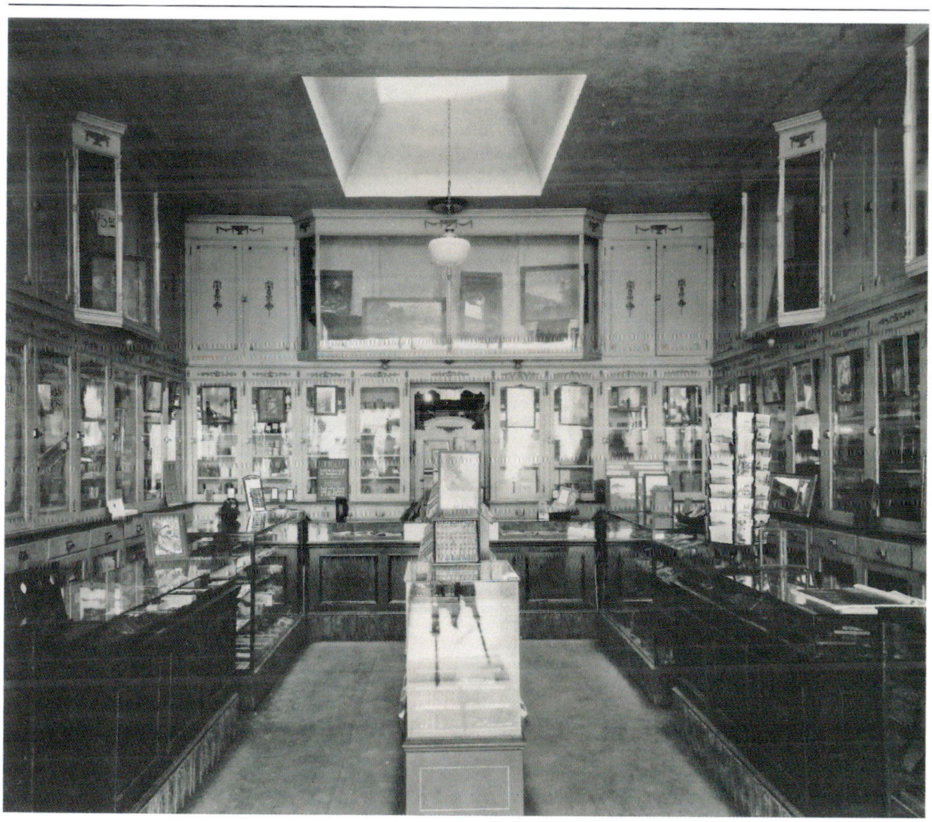

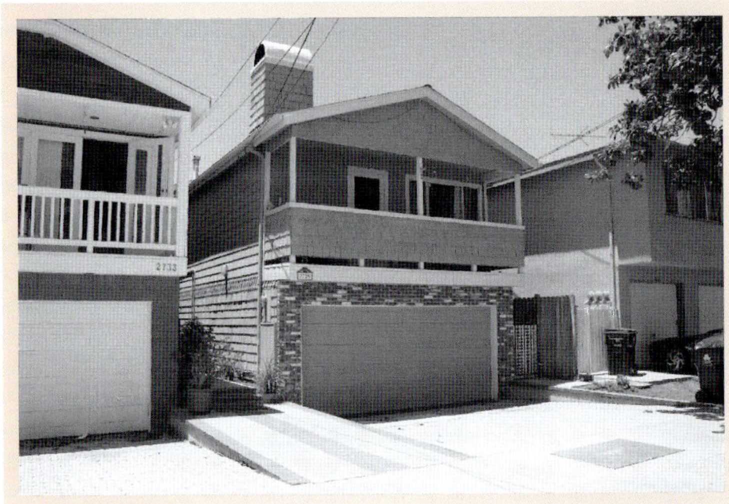

Leach's Barber Shop was once located at 2729 South Pacific Avenue across the street from Fort MacArthur. This was a small, one-chair barbershop that served the community for a number of years. An interior photograph of the shop, not pictured in this book, suggests that Ellis and his wife, Catherine, may have lived in the rear portion of the structure. The photograph below was probably taken between 1931 and 1935. This estimate is based on the National Recovery Administration (NRA) sign in the shop's large window. The NRA was enacted in 1931 but declared unconstitutional by the U.S. Supreme Court in 1935. Membership in the NRA was voluntary, but businesses that did not display its sign were often boycotted. That block of South Pacific Avenue is now filled with apartment buildings and townhouses. The present-day photograph shows a dwelling with the same address of Leach's Barber Shop. At first glance, it is easy to believe it is the same building elevated and with a garage built under it; however, it is an entirely new structure.

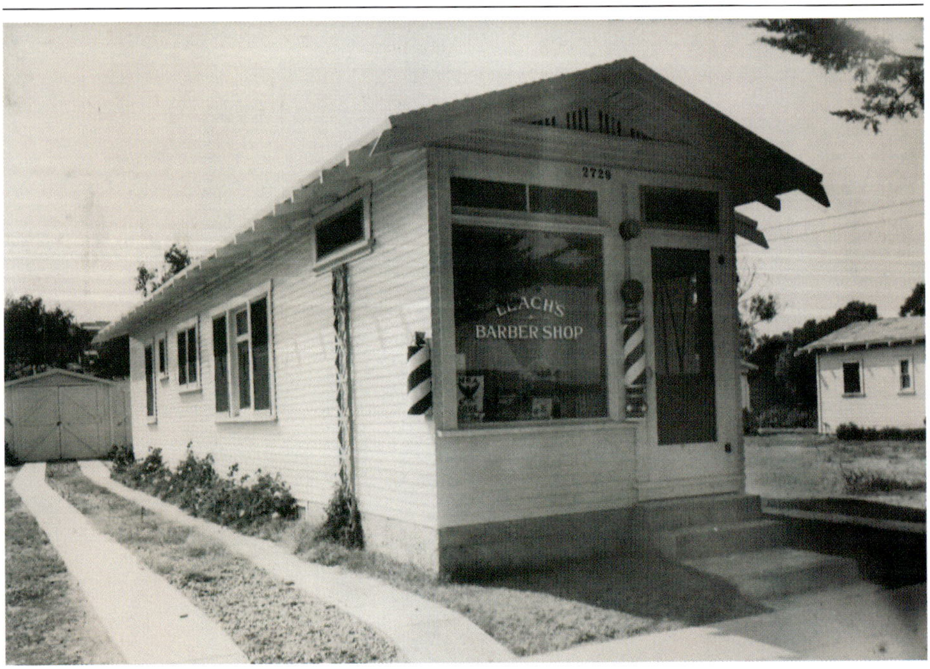

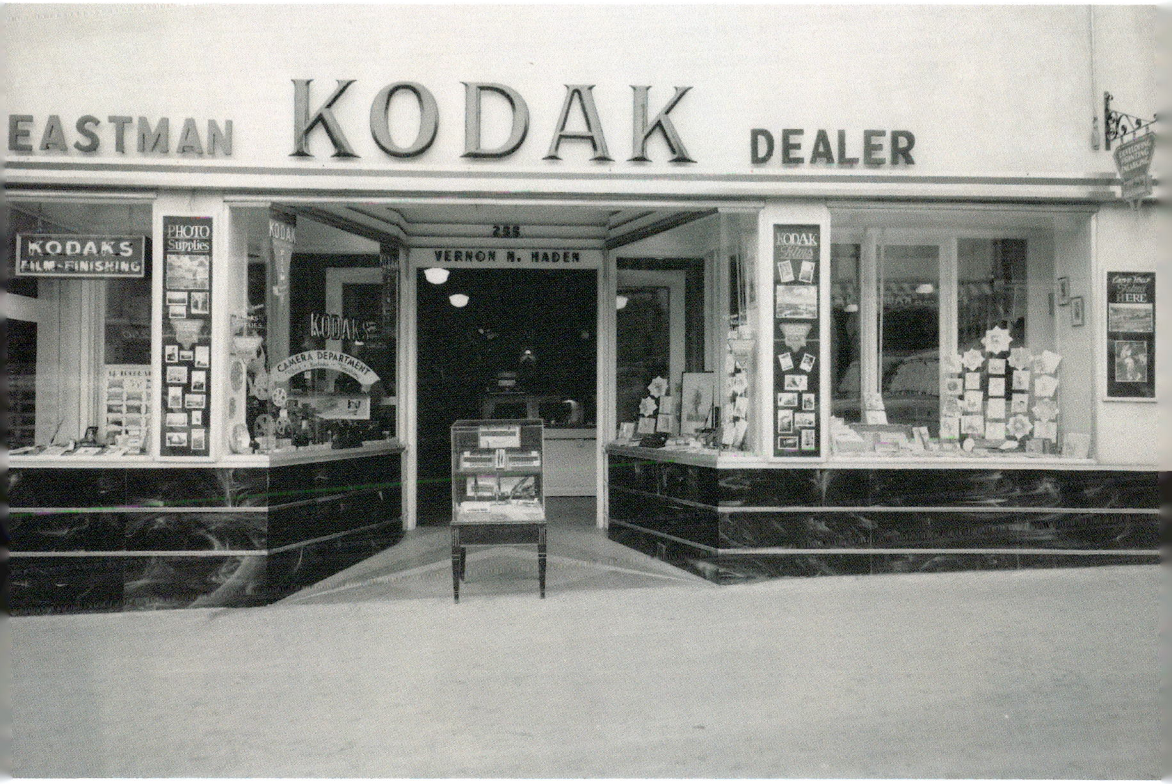

Haden's Photo Shop was located at 255 West Sixth Street when the *c.* 1930 photograph above was taken. Photography supply stores such as Haden's were very popular before drugstores began selling basic photography items, such as film and inexpensive cameras. Its address would suggest it was part of, or near, the now demolished Oxford Hotel building. A company specializing in residential and commercial loans is now at the address in a new building.

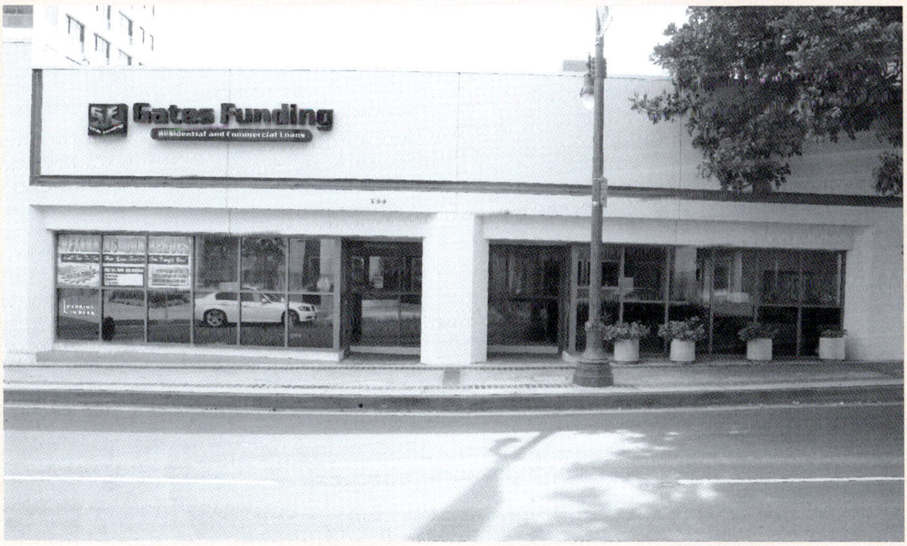

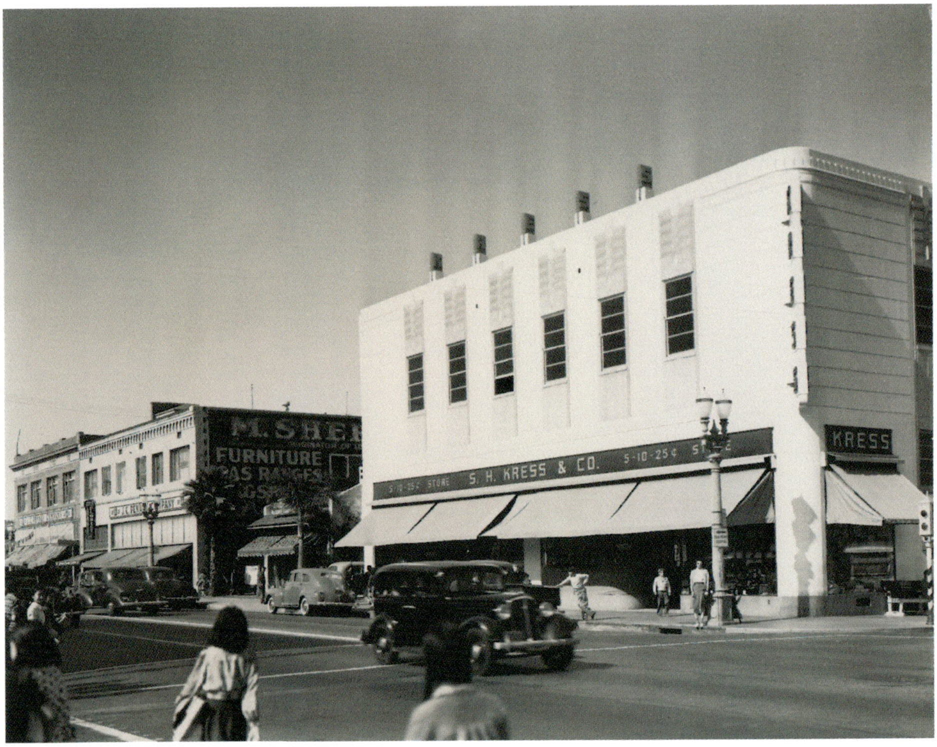

Hundreds of the popular S. H. Kress and Company 5-10-25¢ stores were built in American cities and towns during the early 1900s. The *c.* 1940 photograph above shows the S. H. Kress store on the northeast corner of Seventh Street and Pacific Avenue. To the immediate north of the Kress building (left) was a J. C. Penney store. The buildings that housed these iconic businesses have not been demolished, but their original tenants are gone. The Kress building became a storage facility at some point, with storefronts on the first level. The old J. C. Penney building on Sixth Street and Pacific Avenue presently houses various businesses. Notice in the vintage photograph that the traffic signal on the far right does not have a yellow light.

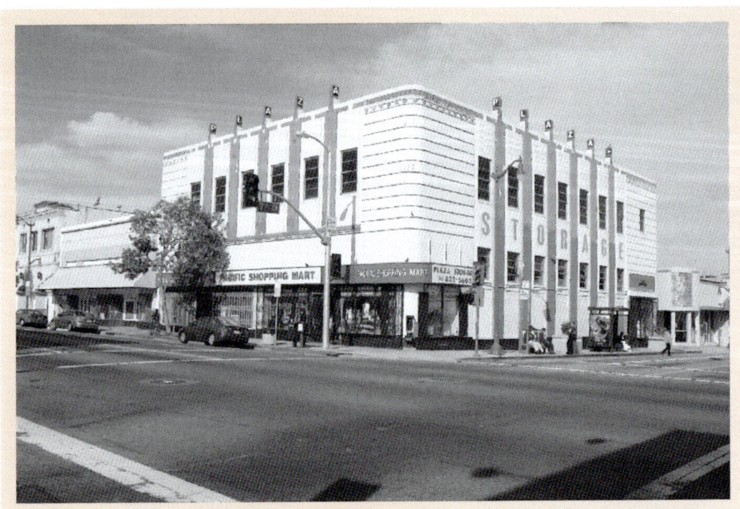

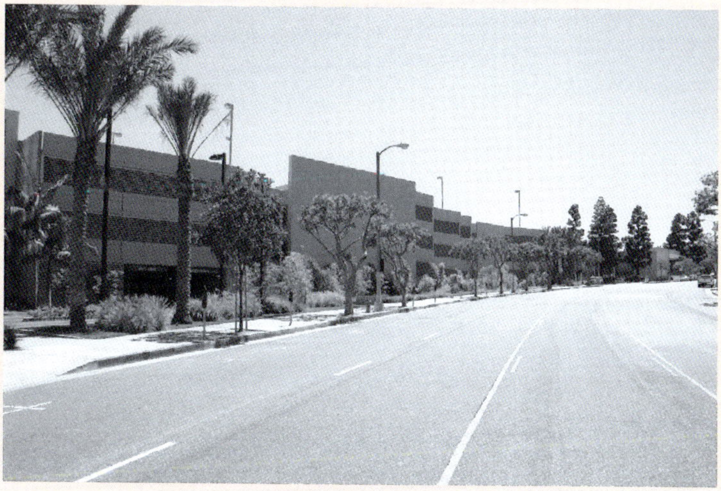

The land that the Saint Francis Hotel occupied was part of a project to lower the elevation of certain areas in San Pedro. The below photograph taken on March 10, 1925, shows the Saint Francis Hotel building propped up as workers dig out ground from underneath it. On the far right of the image can be seen part of the northern section of Fifth Street School, which was torn down two years later. Now occupying the south side of the 200 block of Fifth Street is a large condominium complex. The street has been widened and now swerves slightly to the north. On the far right of the present-day photograph, one can see the northern section of the Los Angeles Superior Courthouse, which was built on the site of Fifth Street School.

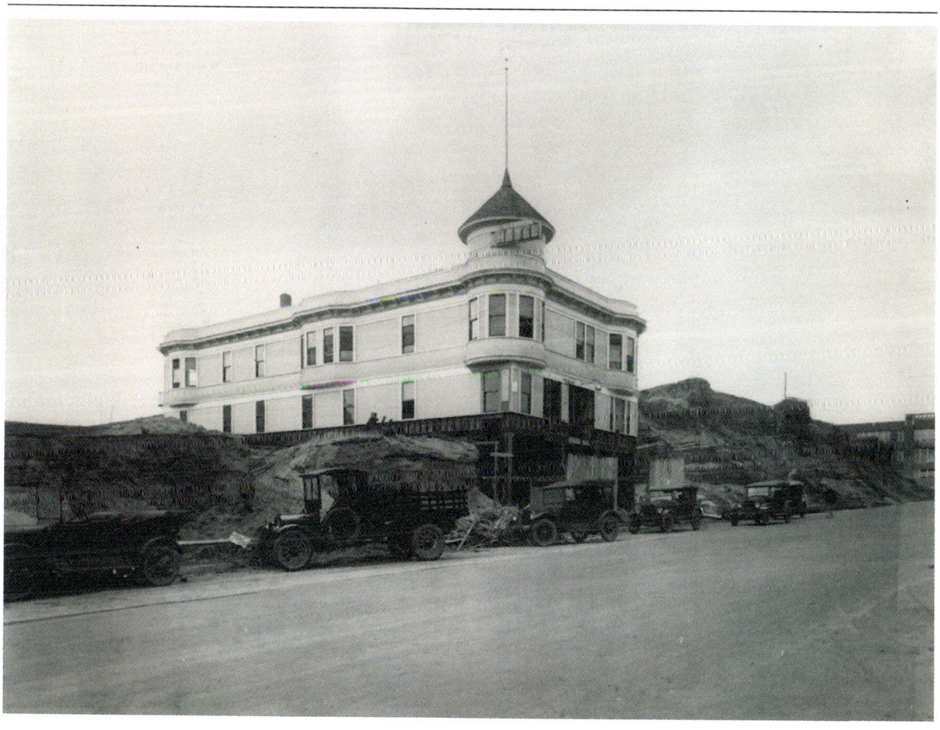

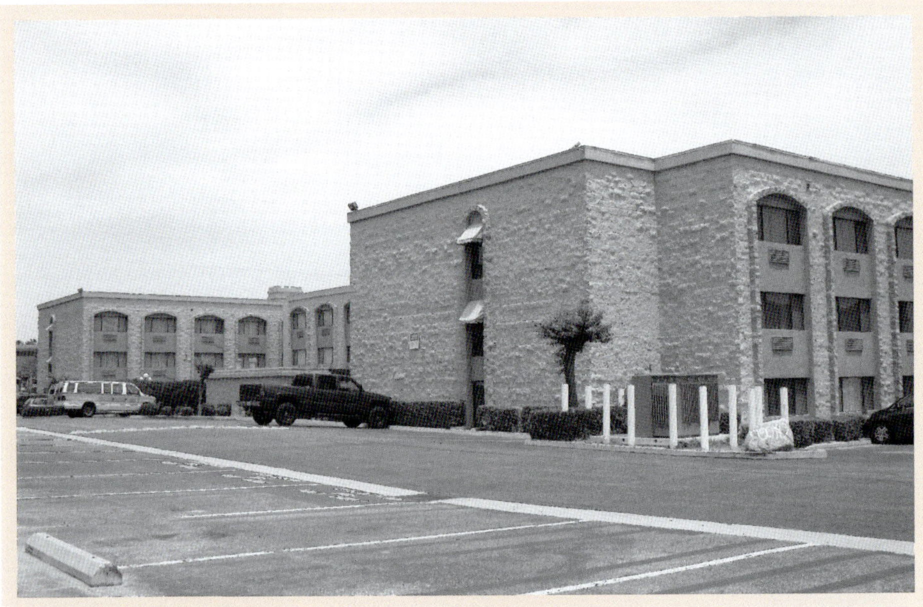

The Alexander Hotel was bordered by Harbor Boulevard (formerly Front Street) on the east and Beacon Street on the west. The 1906 photograph below shows the Beacon Street side of the hotel. The offices of the *San Pedro News* and *Los Angeles Examiner* newspapers are located in the building at the lower right corner of the photograph. Horse-drawn carriages are parked in front of the Alexander. Wires for the electric streetcar system are hanging above the streets. Directly across the street was the Bank of San Pedro. The Sunrise Hotel presently occupies that site. Beacon Street no longer accommodates through traffic at this point, as it once did.

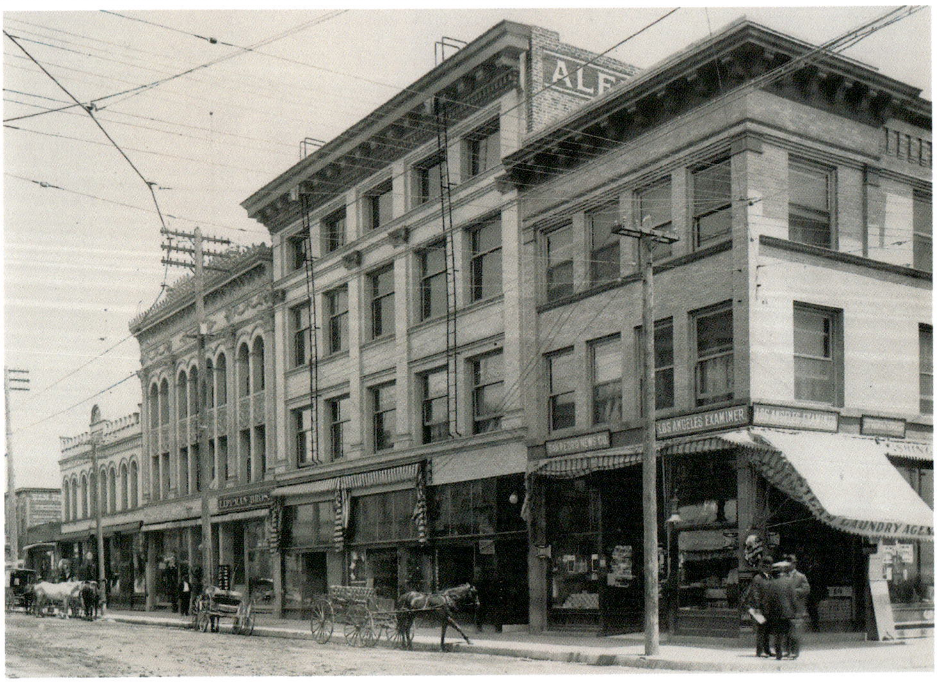

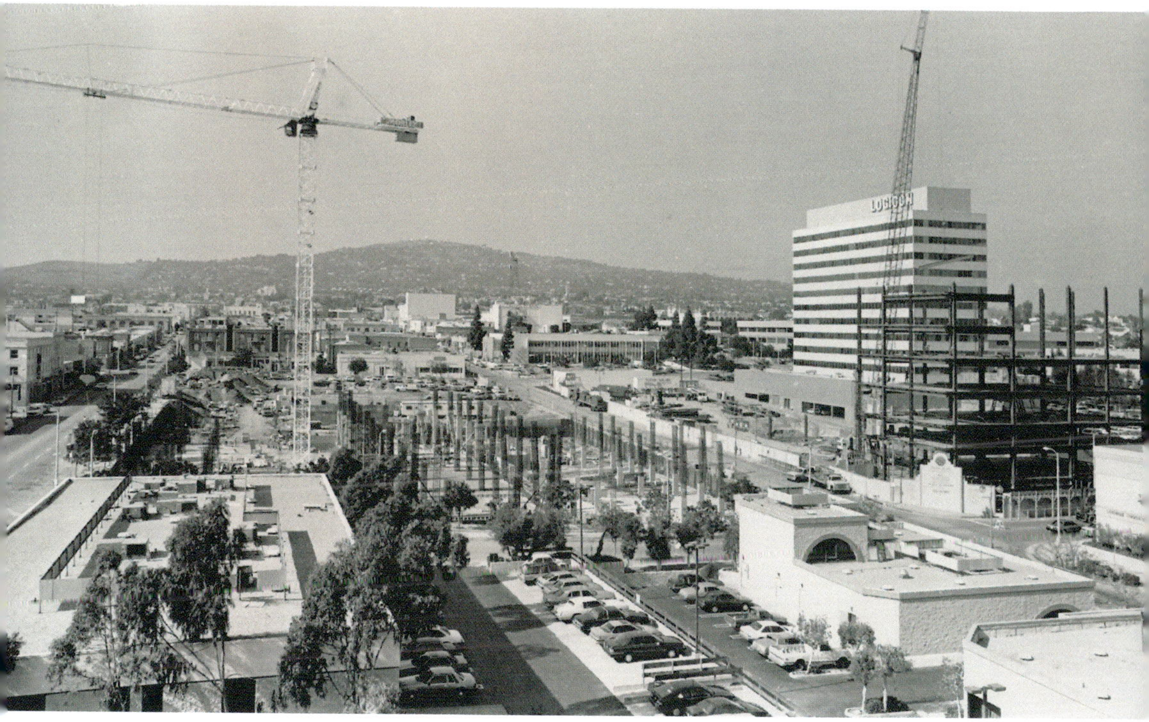

The 1989 photograph above shows the Sheraton Hotel (now the Crowne Plaza Hotel and Resort) under construction on South Palos Verdes Street between Sixth and Seventh Streets. The main structure is being built on land where the Hotel Fern and Bank of Italy (now known as the Bank of America) once stood. On the far right, construction has started on the Northrop Grumman building. The Globe Theatre was on that property. The Logicon building on the right was San Pedro's tallest building until it was demolished to make room for a condominium complex. Buildings in the foreground of the present-day photograph were once sites of the A. P. Ferl and Anderson buildings.

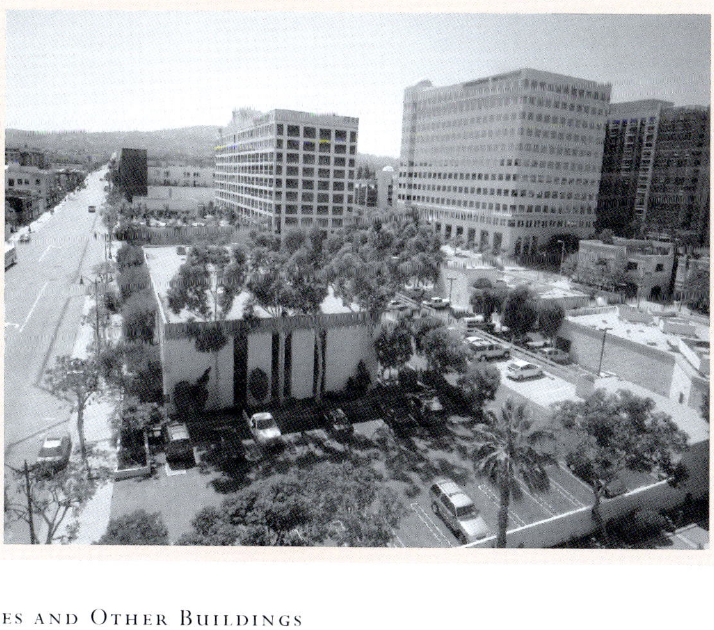

When built in 1912, this ornate theater featured the entertainment of choice at the time—vaudeville. As the popularity of vaudeville faded, the Globe was converted to a silent movie house. Sound equipment was installed in the late 1920s when talkies became the moneymaker for movie theaters. In its last years of existence, the Globe became an adult movie house. It was demolished in 1971 as part of a redevelopment project. The Northrop Grumman building now occupies the site.

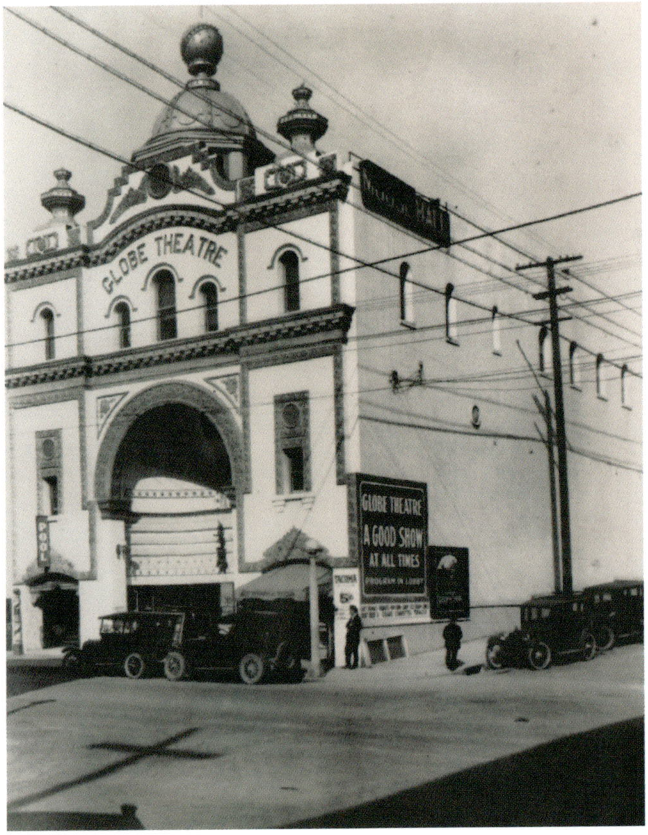

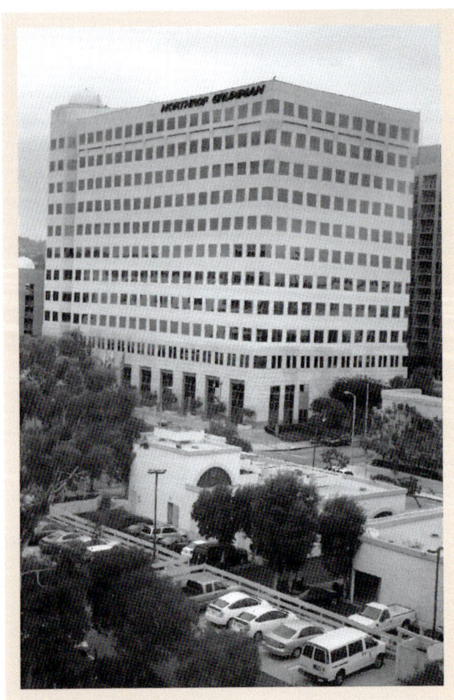

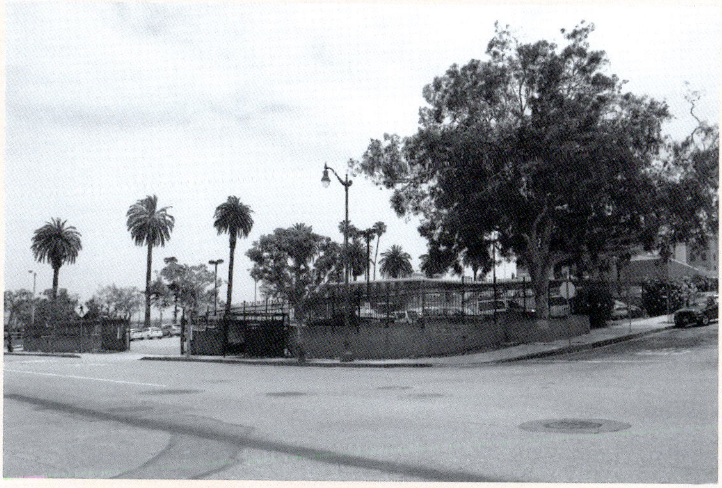

The majestic Fox Cabrillo Theater stood on the south side of Seventh Street between Beacon and Palos Verdes Streets from 1923 to January 1961. This theater could seat over 1,500 moviegoers. Features showing when the 1937 photograph below was taken were: *Camille*, staring Greta Garbo and Robert Taylor, and *Off to the Races*, starring Slim Summerville. The building also housed offices of the Union Pacific Railroad and Western Union, as well as a soda fountain on the first floor. There was a billiard hall and a dentist who went by the name of "Painless Parker" on the second floor. Today this property is a parking lot for Los Angeles City employees.

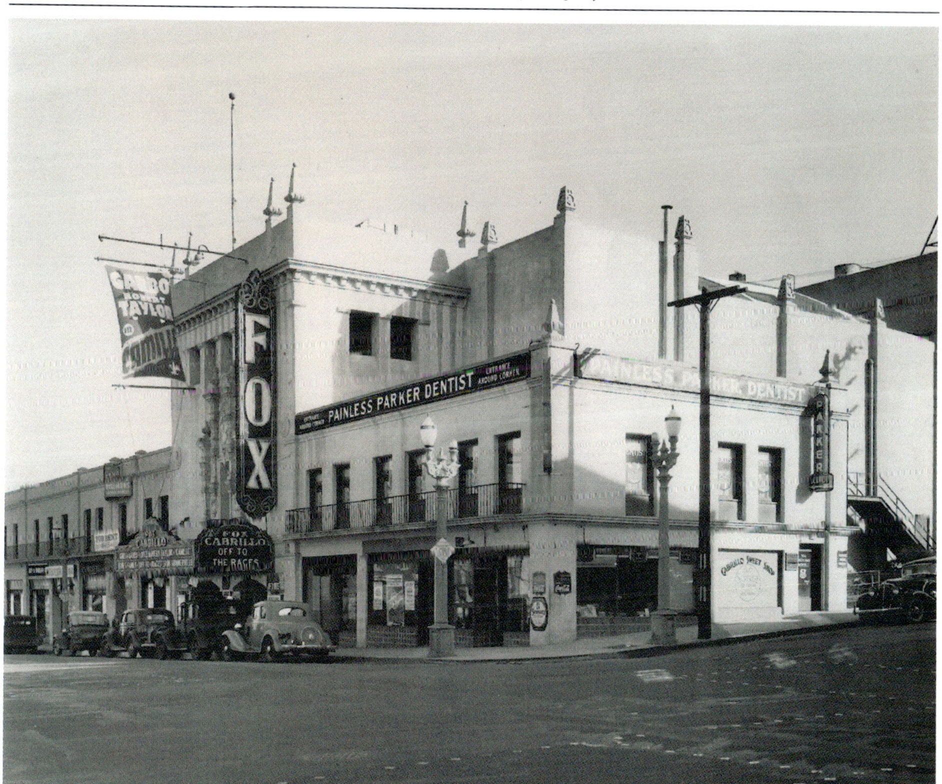

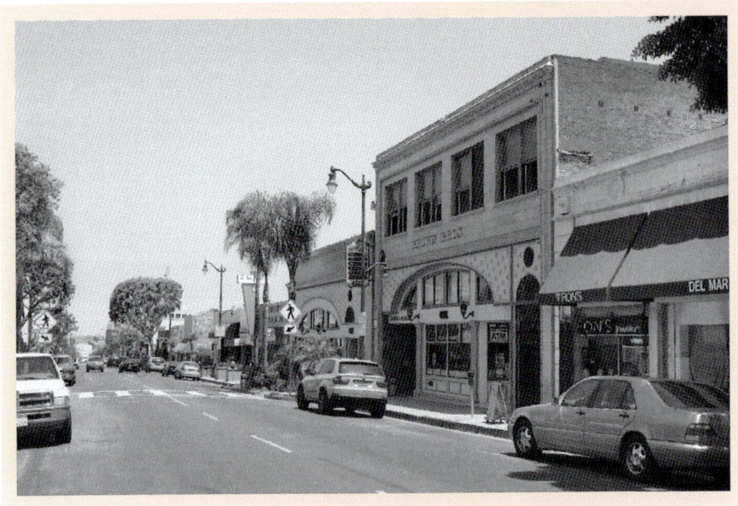

The Brown Brothers building is located on the south side of Sixth Street on the first block east of South Pacific Avenue. The building's original ornate roof decorations are seen in the 1929 photograph below. They probably were removed because of damage sustained during the 1933 Long Beach earthquake. The building is still standing and is still in use today. It houses a variety of small businesses. The structure to the right of Brown Brothers has survived and is now home to a jewelry and hobby store. Del Mar furniture is no longer at that location.

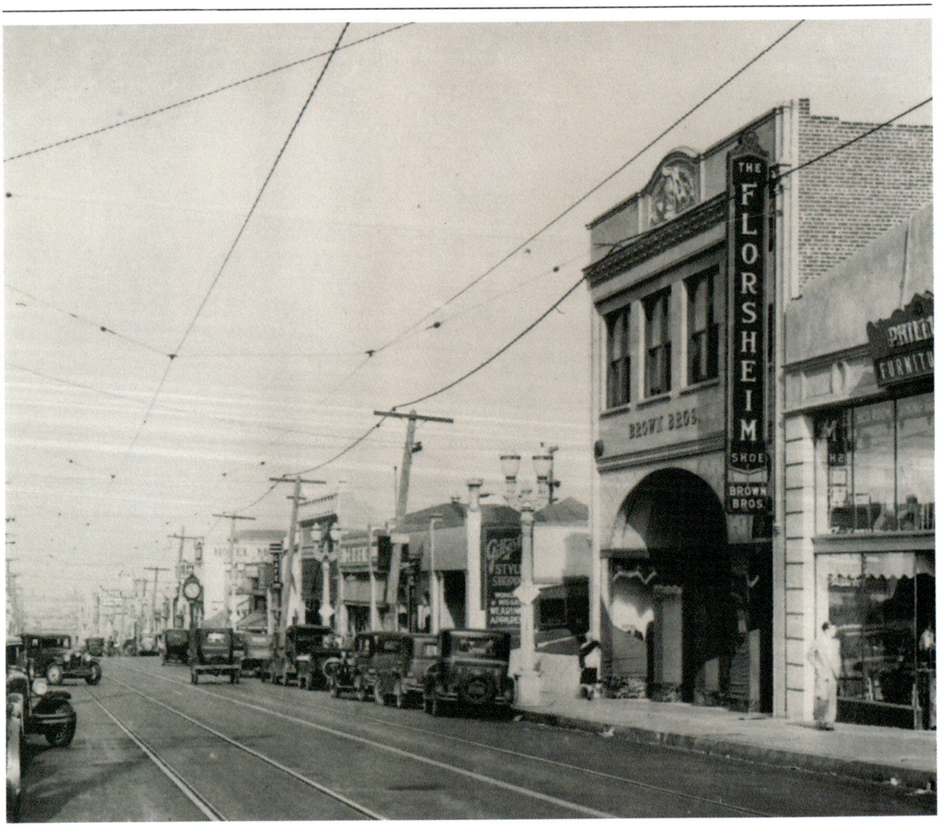

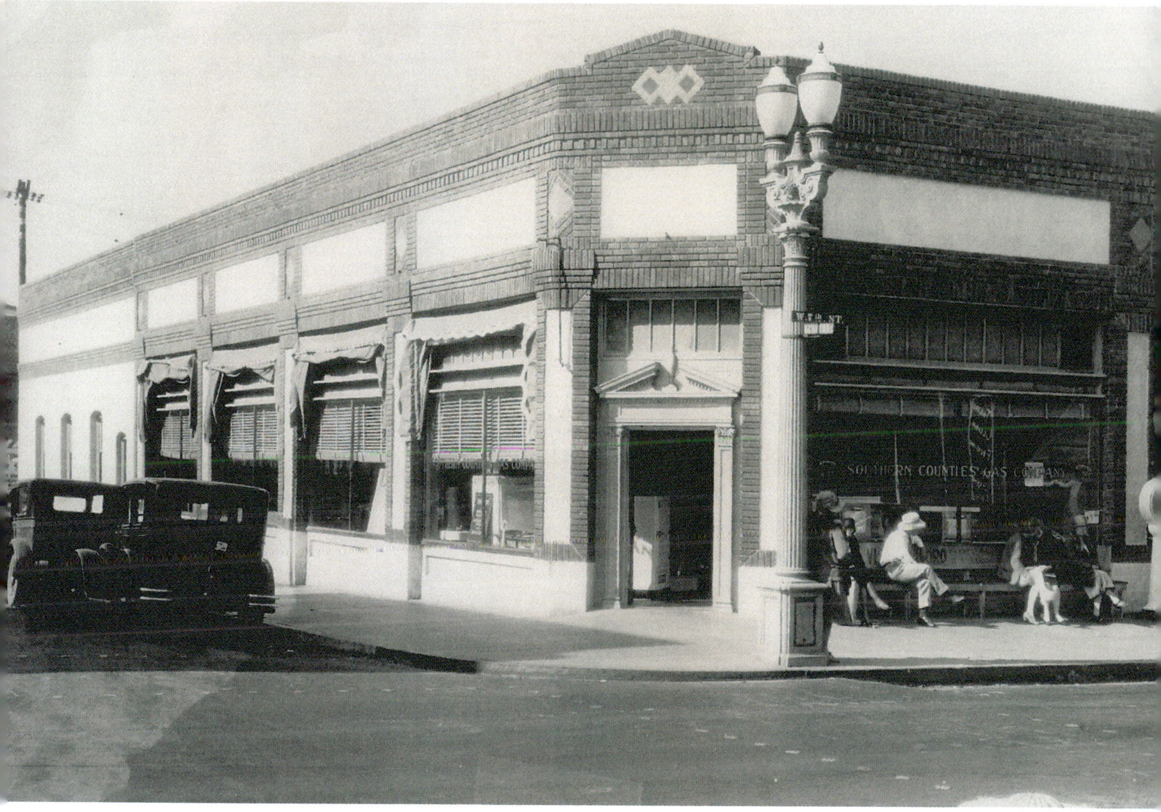

Pictured in the vintage photograph above is the Southern Counties Gas Company located on the northeast corner of Sixth and Centre Streets. It provided natural gas to the San Pedro community. The Centre Street Lofts are presently located on that block. The building features an interactive robot named Mojo that beams a spotlight on people walking by.

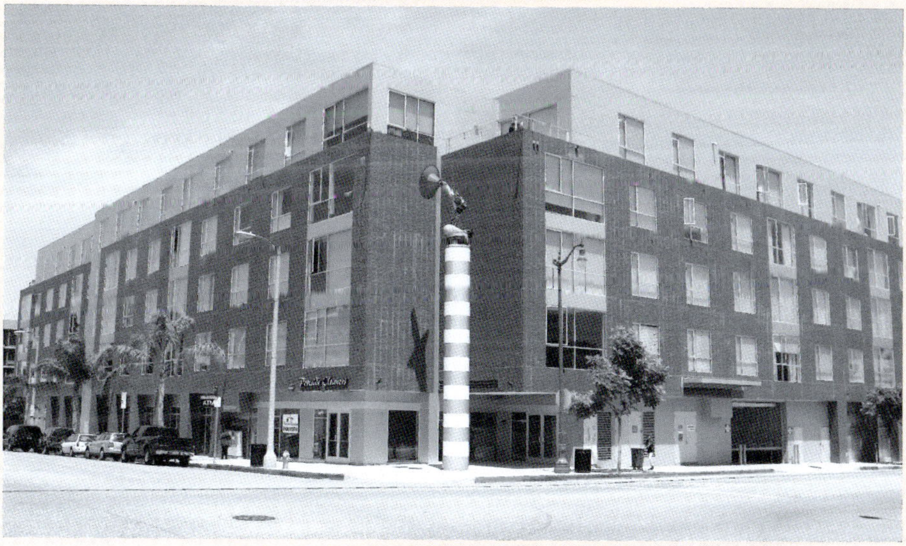

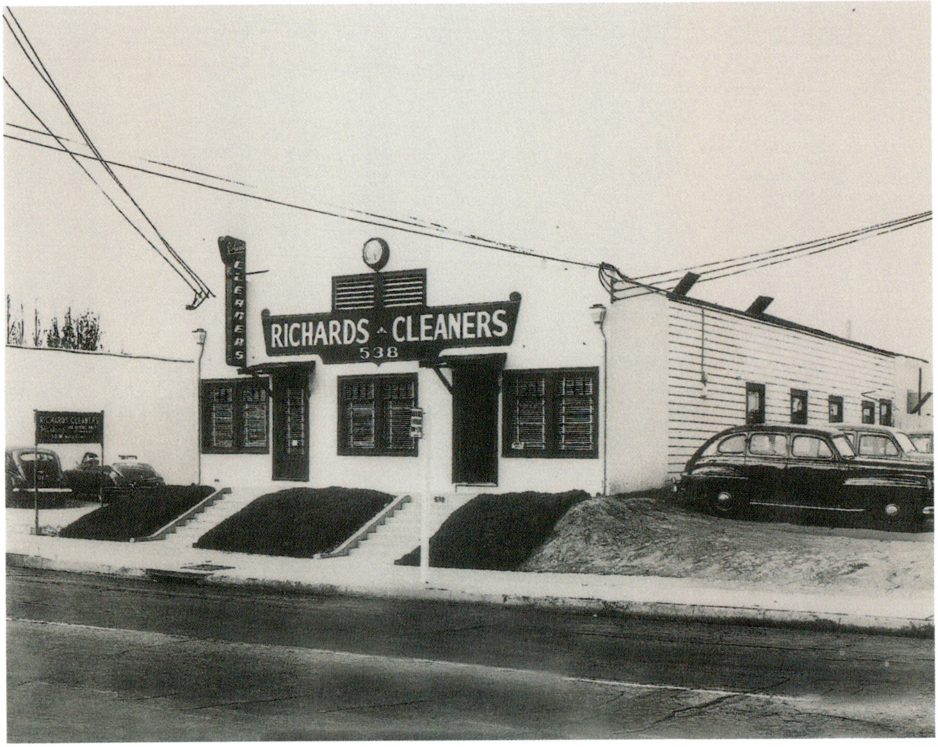

Richard's Cleaners is located on the 500 block of Fifth Street near Pacific Avenue and is one of San Pedro's oldest operating businesses. It has served the San Pedro community since 1904. That was five years before San Pedro was incorporated into the city of Los Angeles. The building has been expanded and renovated since the *c.* 1940 photograph above was taken.

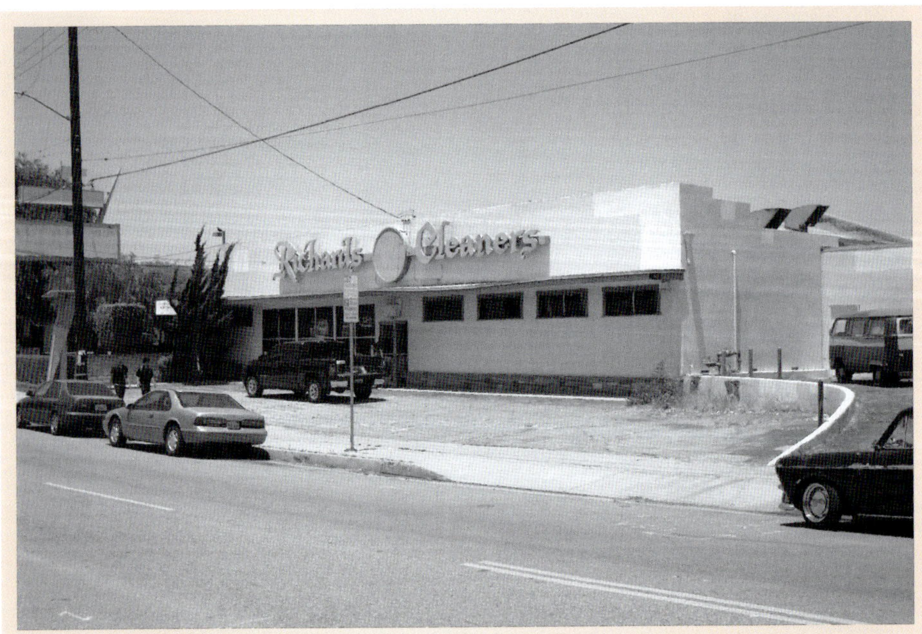

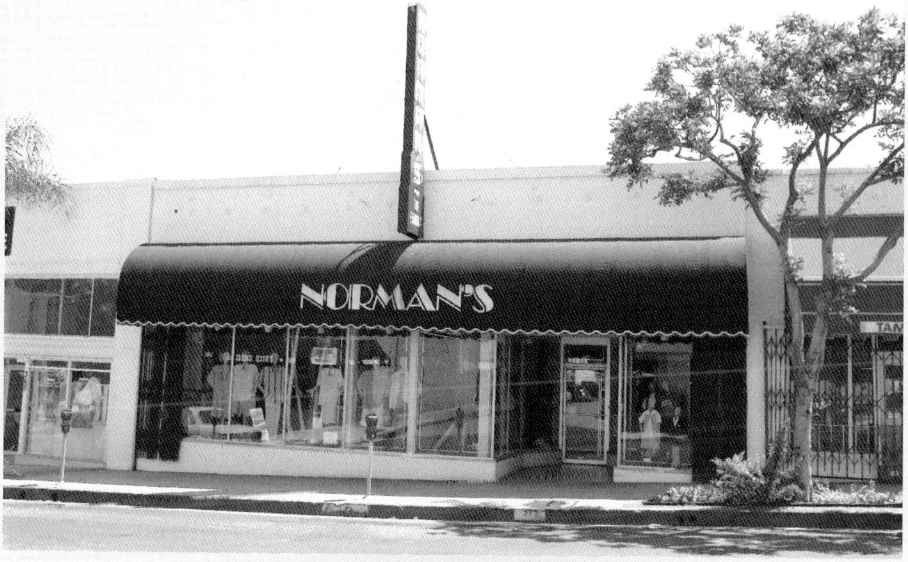

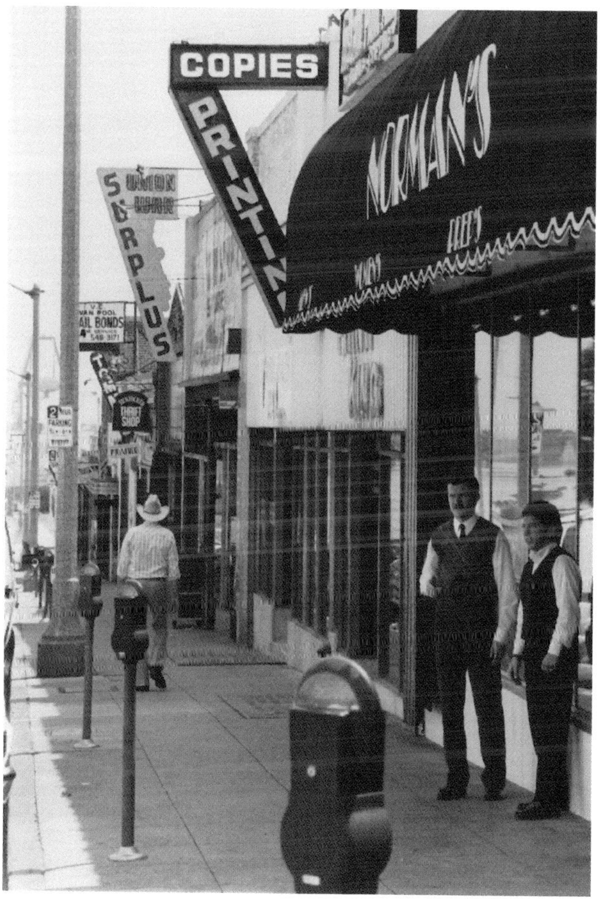

The section of West Sixth Street between South Pacific Avenue and Harbor Boulevard has been the location of many San Pedro businesses. Most are gone now. Norman's Men and Boys Wear, located on the 300 block of West Sixth Street, has been a family-owned and operated business since 1937. Pictured in the photograph at left taken in 1985 are owner Nick D'Ambrosi (left) and his business partner Mike Mazzella. The copy/printing business and Union War Surplus are no longer in business.

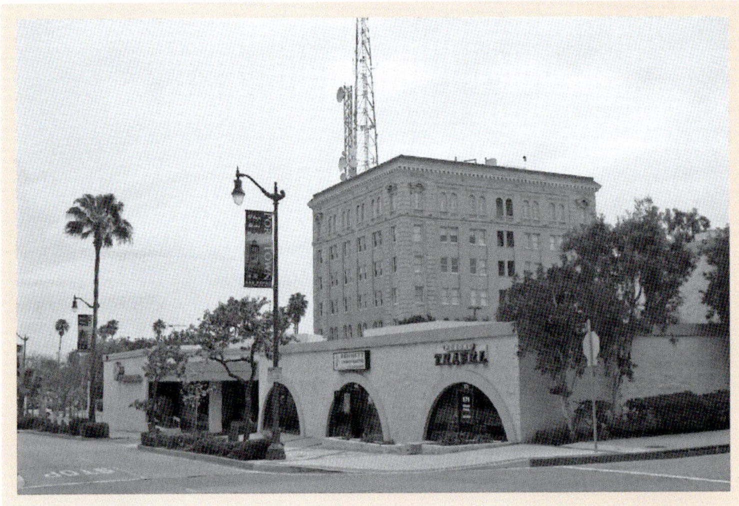

For a period during the 1920s, the southeast corner of the intersection of Sixth and Palos Verdes Streets was the location of the Guaranty Trust and Savings Bank's Harbor Branch (not pictured). Years later, the corner section became the Back Bay Hotel, as seen in the 1971 photograph below. There was an interesting assortment of buildings on the south side of the 100 block of Sixth Street. There were four bars, a college for barmaids and waitresses, a barbershop, and a bookstore. The bar in the foreground is the Farmer's Daughter Saloon Tavern Tabernacle. Its sign reads, "Home of the Irish Mafia to Stamp Out Home Drinking." The top floor of the municipal building is barely visible in the upper center of the photograph. Today the municipal building is the only recognizable landmark in the area. The block was completely demolished during the Beacon Street redevelopment project in the early 1970s. Sixth Street was narrowed, and the sidewalk was widened.

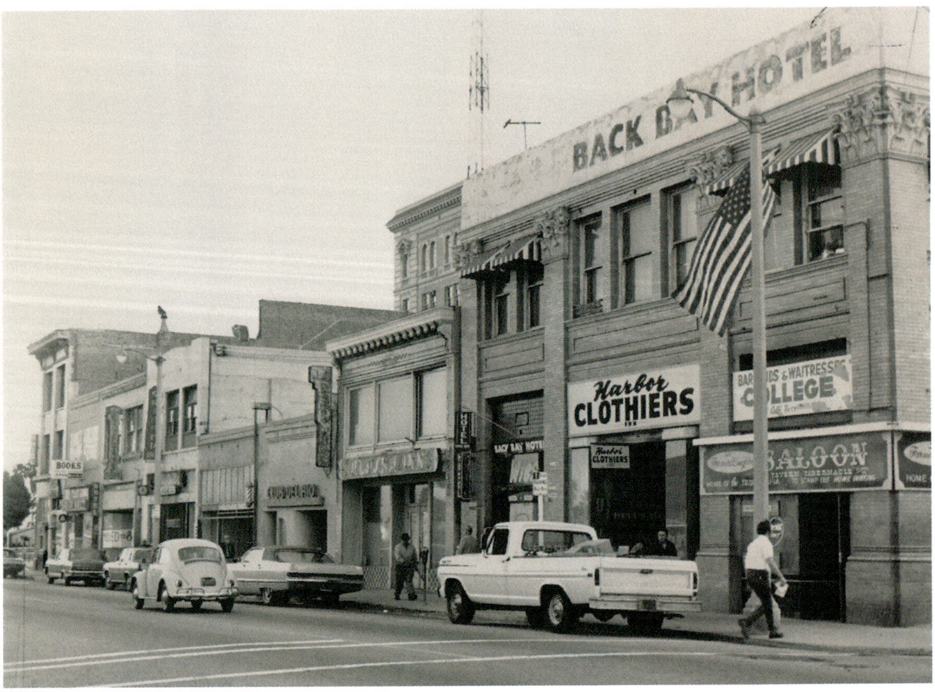

CHAPTER 5

SAN PEDRO AT PLAY

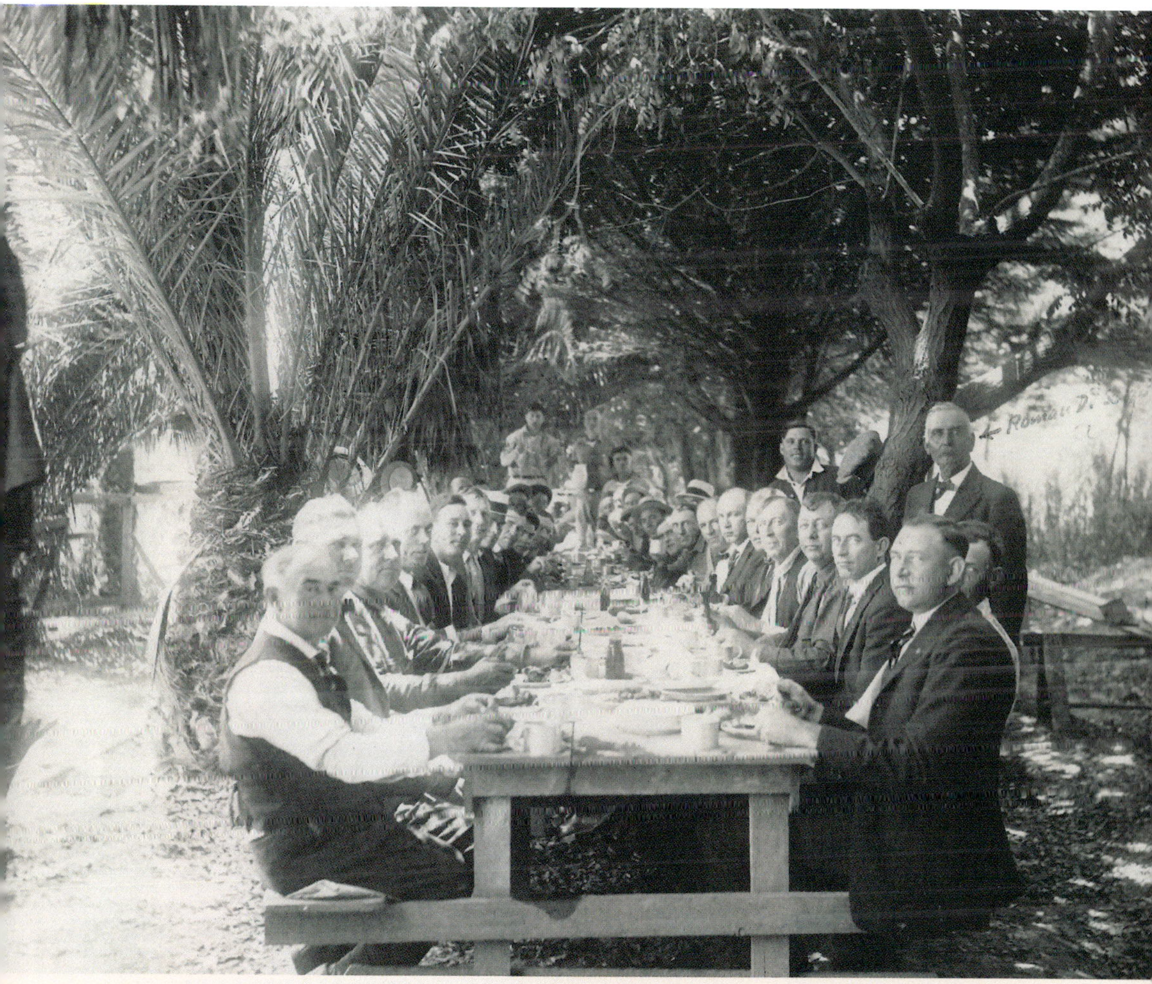

Land developer Roman D. Sepulveda (standing at right) is seen entertaining a few of his friends at White Point on June 18, 1922. These were probably some of San Pedro's most influential and powerful business leaders.

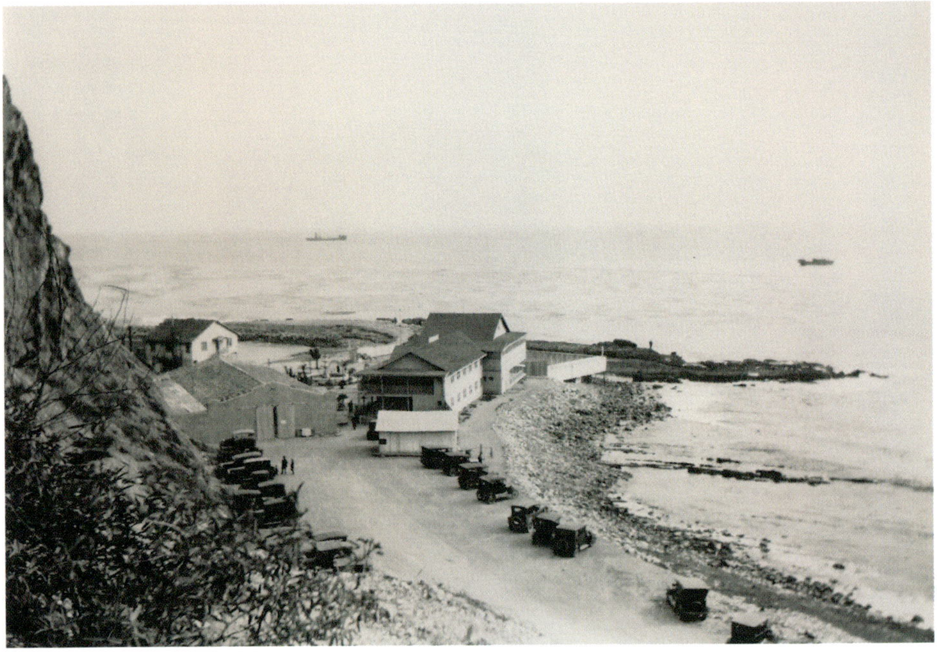

On June 14, 1925, the above photograph was taken of the White Point Hot Springs Hotel and Spa. To the right of the hotel can be seen a portion of its famous Olympic hot springs swimming pool. Brothers Tojuro and Tamiji Tagami and Ramon Sepulveda built access roads to the area and dug out the hot springs. During the 1920s, this was a very popular beach resort, especially among Japanese-Americans. Natural disasters (such as the 1933 Long Beach earthquake that sealed up the natural hot spring vent that fed the pool), the Great Depression, and political events led to the closing of the resort. All that remains in the area named Royal Palms County Beach are pieces of the hot springs pool and the parking lot. When the tide is right, present-day visitors can smell sulfur. The fountain that was in front of the hotel has been brought up to street level and is part of a recently constructed recreational area.

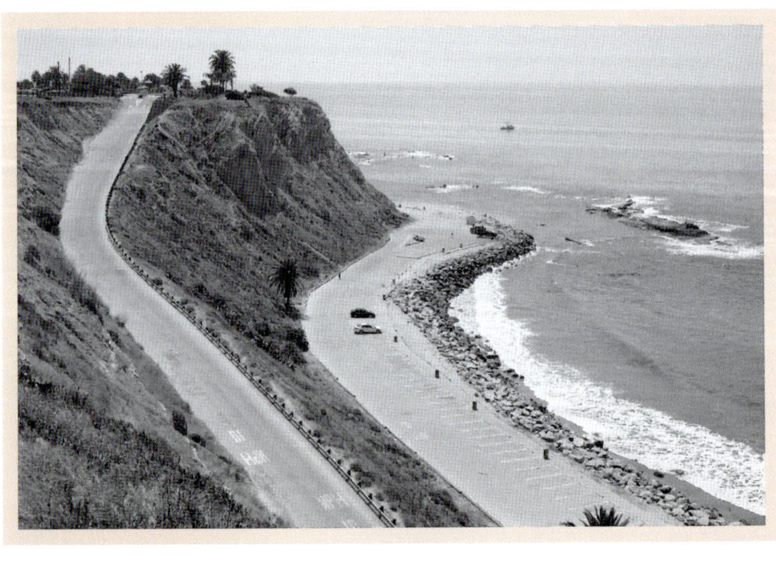

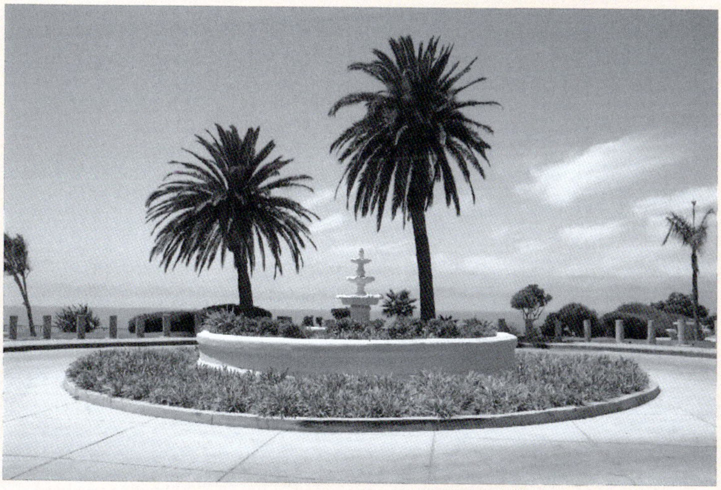

The White Point Hot Springs Hotel and Spa opened on August 6, 1922. The photograph below of a young girl and dog in front of the resort's fountain was taken three years later. She might be a member of the founding family of White Point Hot Springs Resort, the Tagami family. Roman Sepulveda was also a founder of this recreational facility. It was partially buried at its original location and was brought up to street level piece by piece in the 1980s. The fountain, restored to its original splendor, presently marks the entrance to Royal Palms State Beach on West Paseo Del Mar near South Western Avenue.

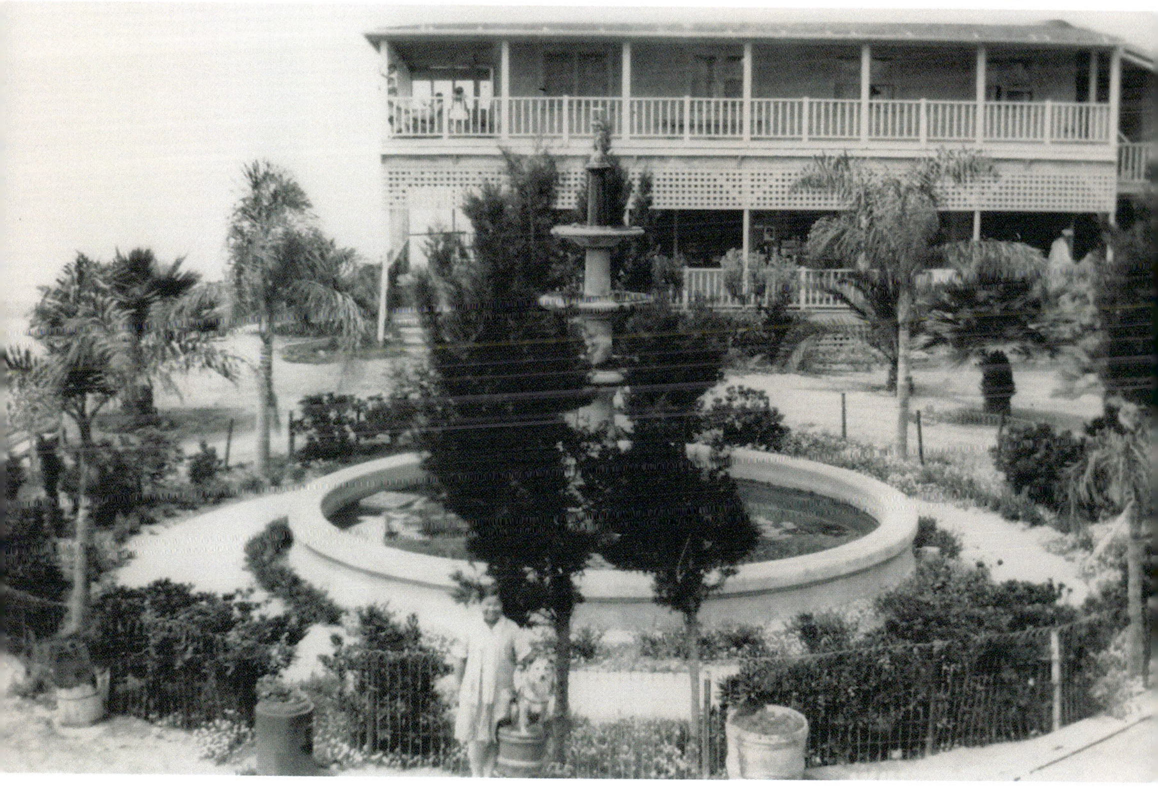

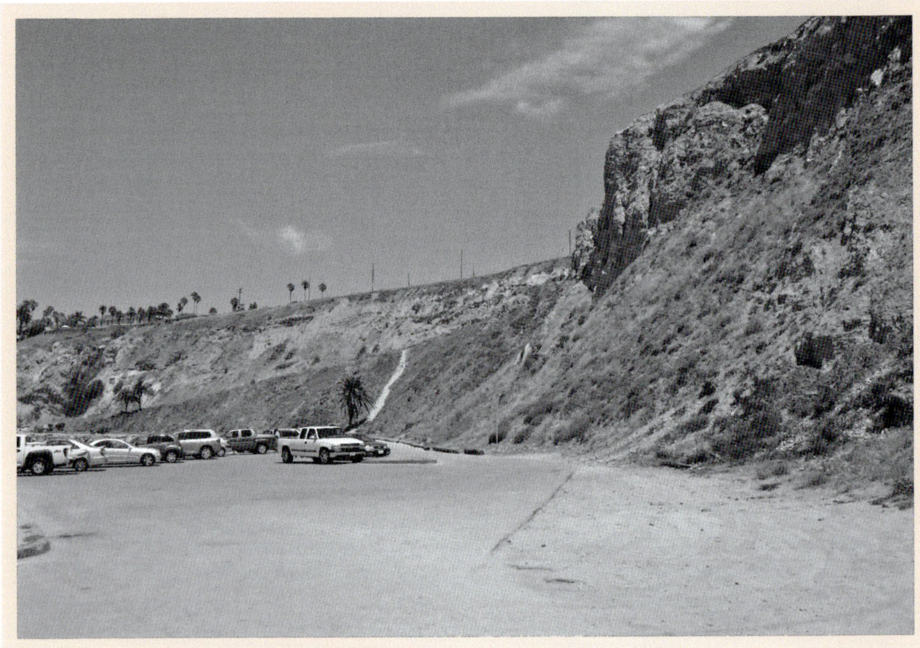

Taken on June 14, 1925, the photograph below gives an up-close view of the hotel and fountain of the White Point Hot Springs Resort and Spa site. A number of factors led to the closing of this resort, which was very popular with the Japanese population. The hotel and spas are gone, but the fountain has been moved to street level as part of a new park's entrance.

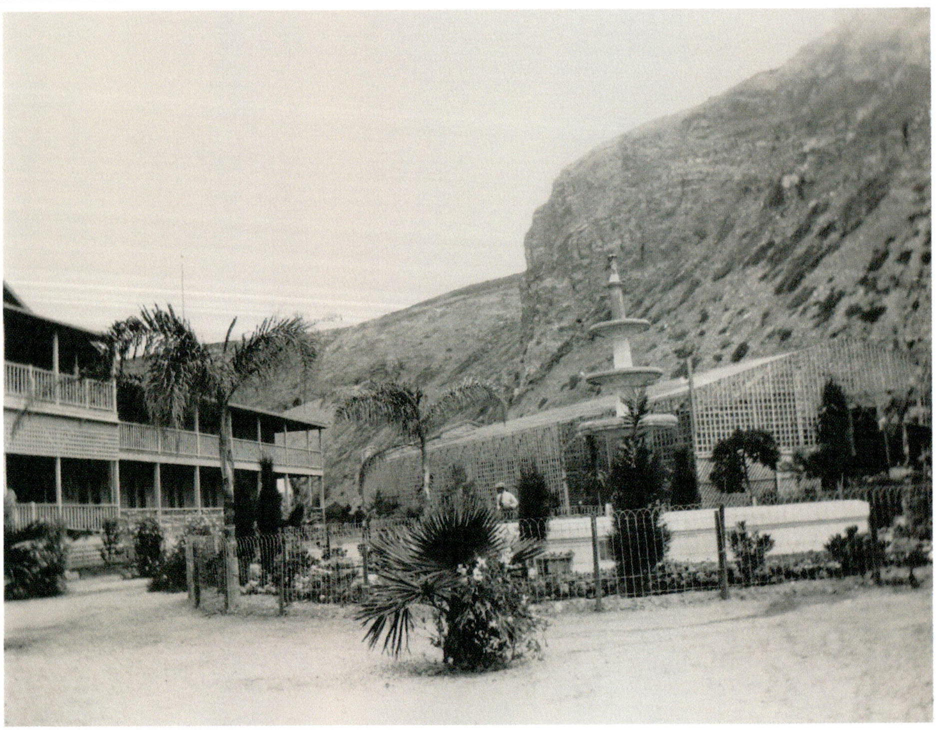

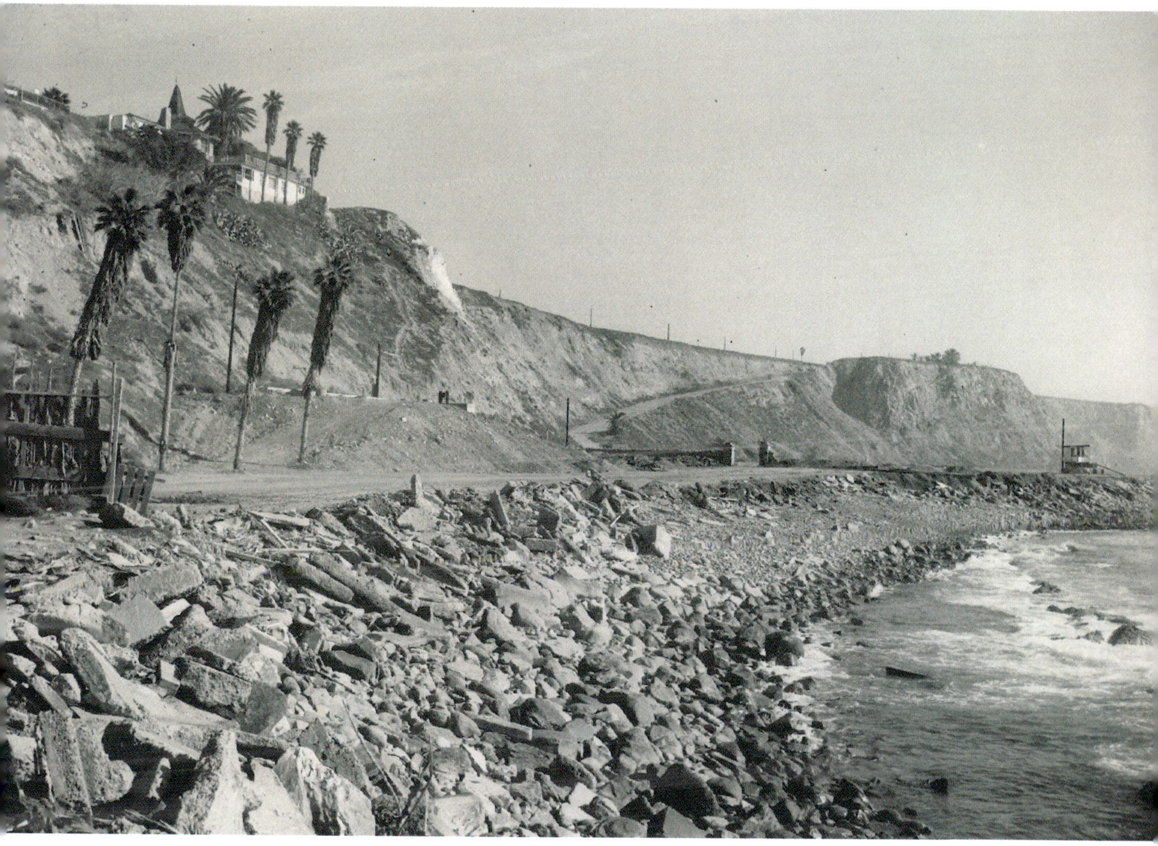

The date of the photograph above is unknown. It shows that at one time there was a stone wall to the entrance of Royal Palms. In the upper left of the image is the Gate House, with its inverted coned roof. A significant amount of land has eroded away near that house and the area of the access road. Only traces of the stone wall entrance remain. Royal Palms State Beach is still a pleasure for tourists.

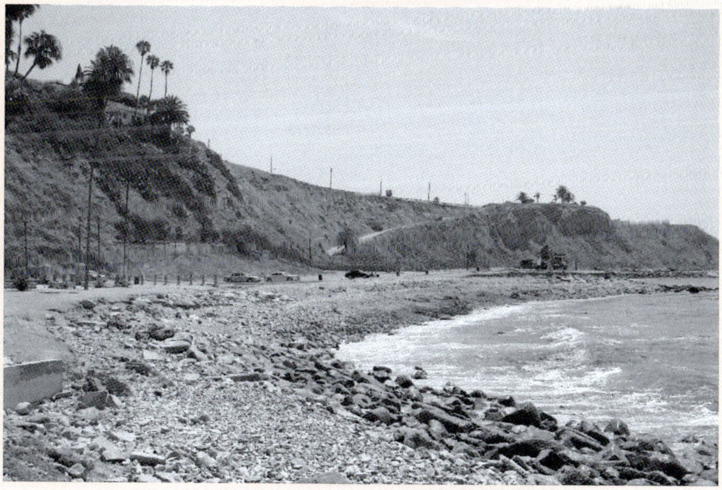

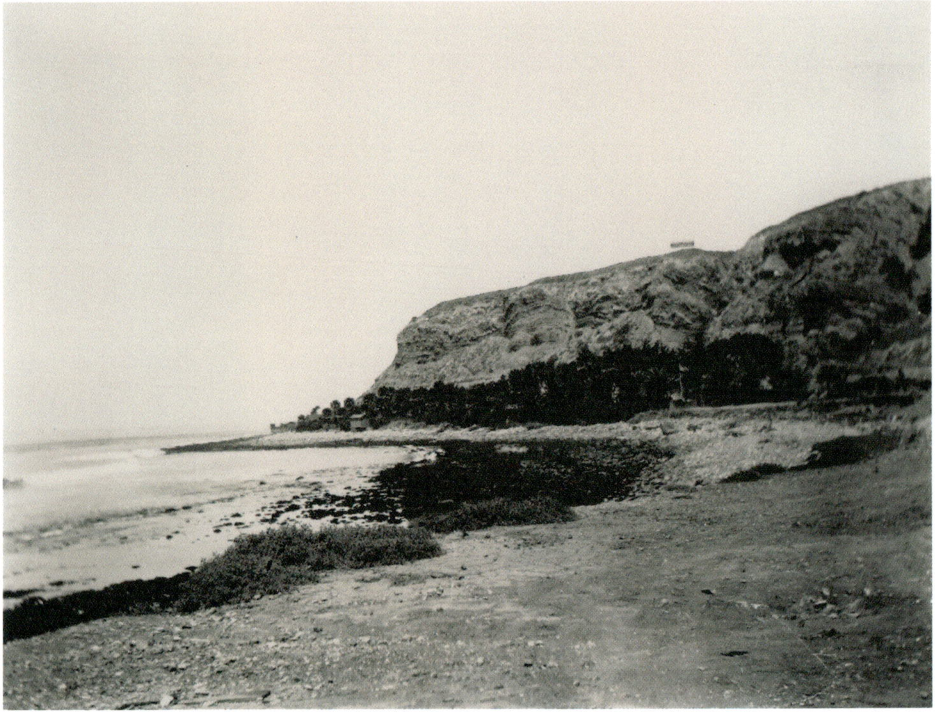

Taken on May 3, 1923, the photograph above shows Sepulveda Park (Royal Palms). Roman Sepulveda entertained friends, such as George H. Peck, at this scenic location. The area above the park was Sepulveda's golf course. The present-day photograph shows that the park, now Royal Palms State Beach, is still in use today. Houses have been built on the land that was once the site of the golf course.

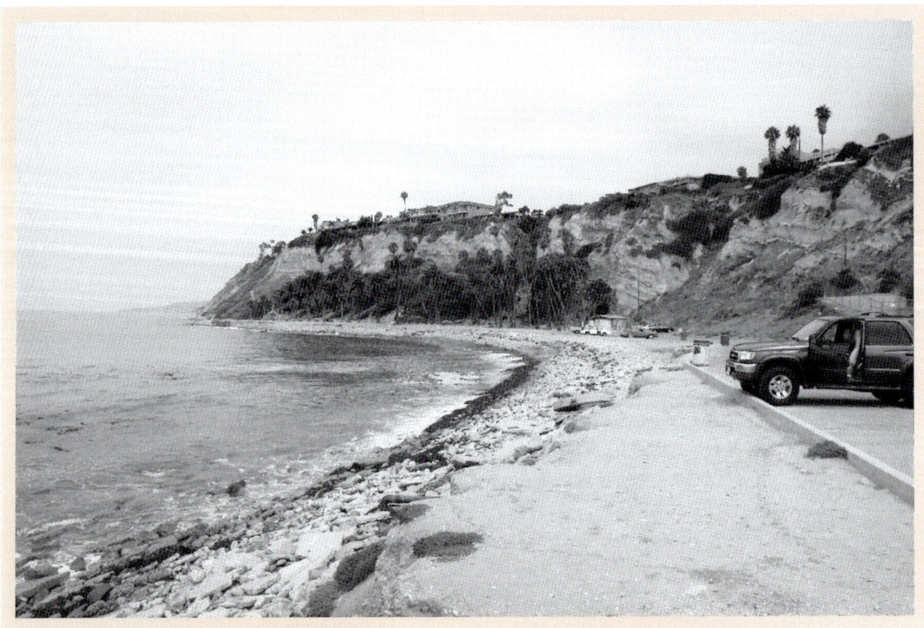

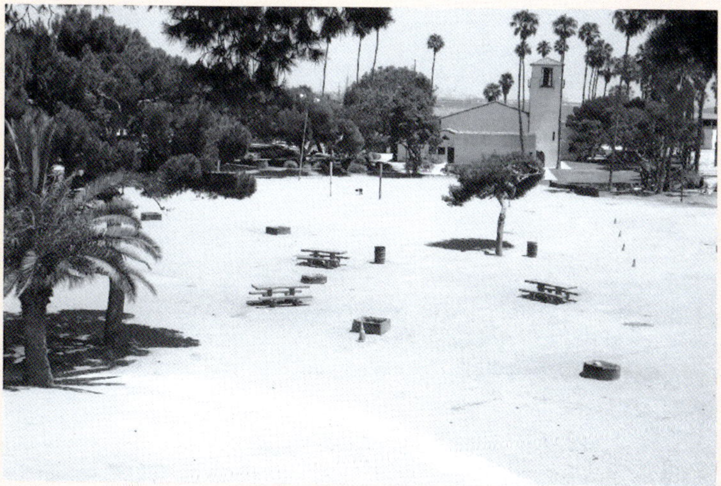

The undated photograph below shows the iconic Cabrillo Beach Bath House that was built in 1932 as a destination for people riding the Pacific Electric streetcar from Los Angeles to spend a day at the beach. For 10¢, they could rent a swimming suit and towel for the day. The bathhouse and the boathouse in the center of the photograph were both used during the 1932 Olympic Games. The bathhouse still stands and provides educational activities and classes, along with changing and shower areas for men and women. The Cabrillo Beach Museum, which was once housed in the bathhouse, moved to a separate building in 1981. The boathouse was demolished in the 1970s.

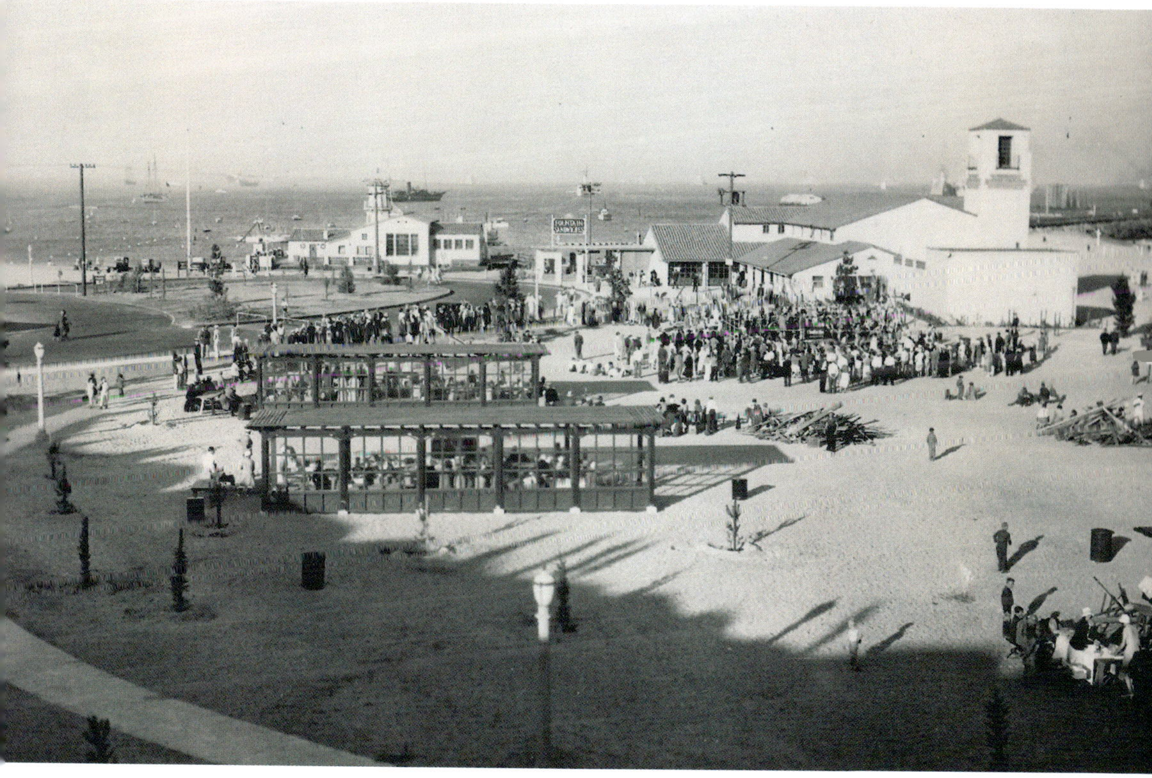

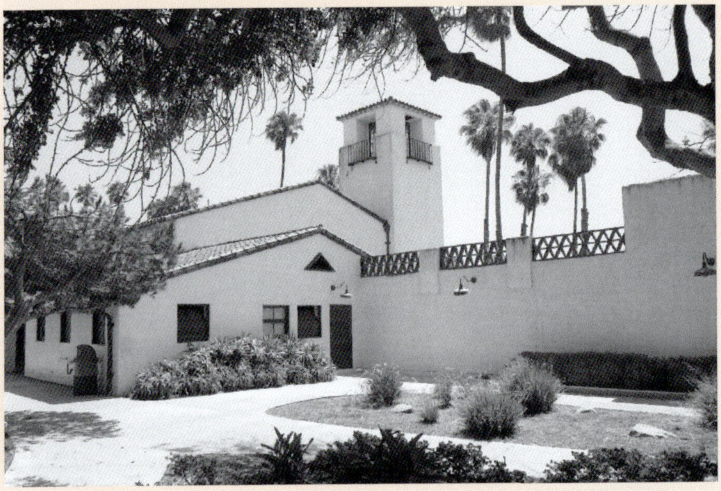

The Cabrillo Beach Bath House was still under construction in the 1931 photograph below. This building is the only remaining example of the bathhouses that were once common at Southern California beaches. The bathhouse was home to the Cabrillo Beach Museum until 1981, when the museum moved to a larger separate facility a few yards from the bathhouse. The structure's exterior has hardly changed since it opened in 1932.

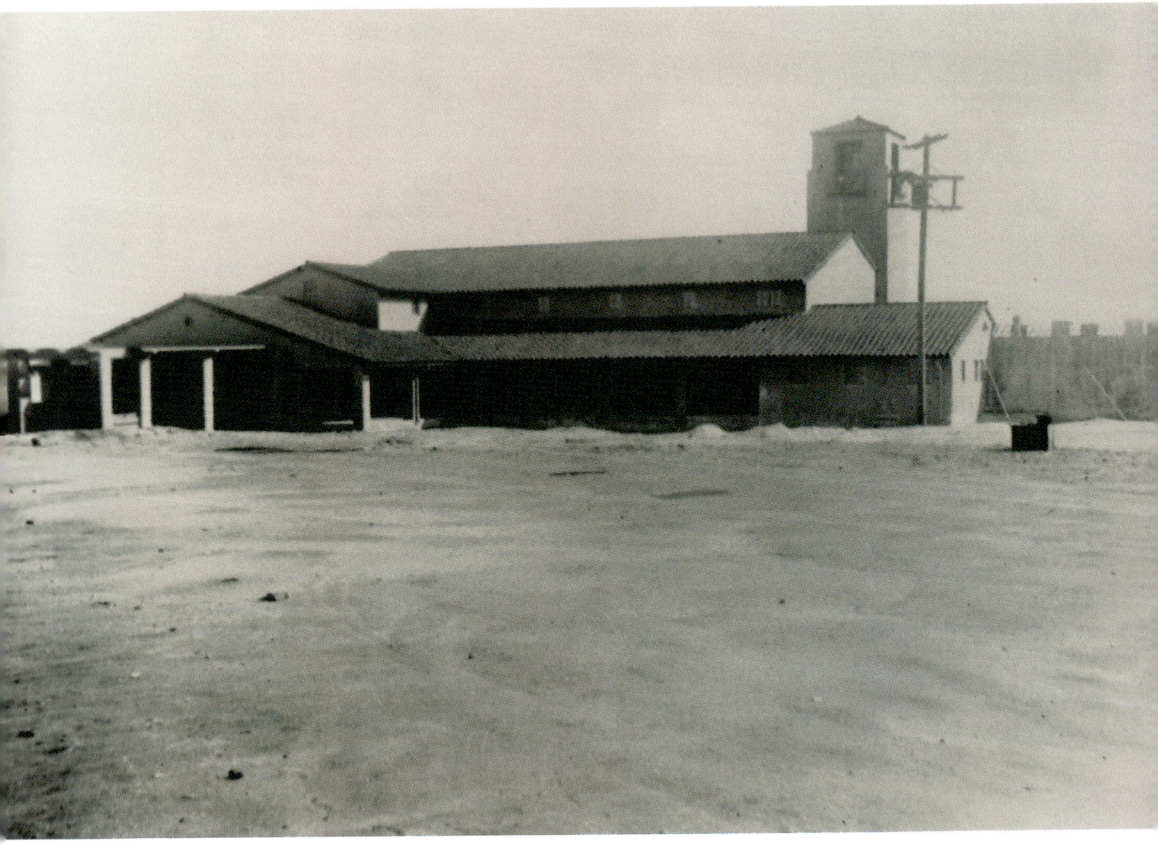

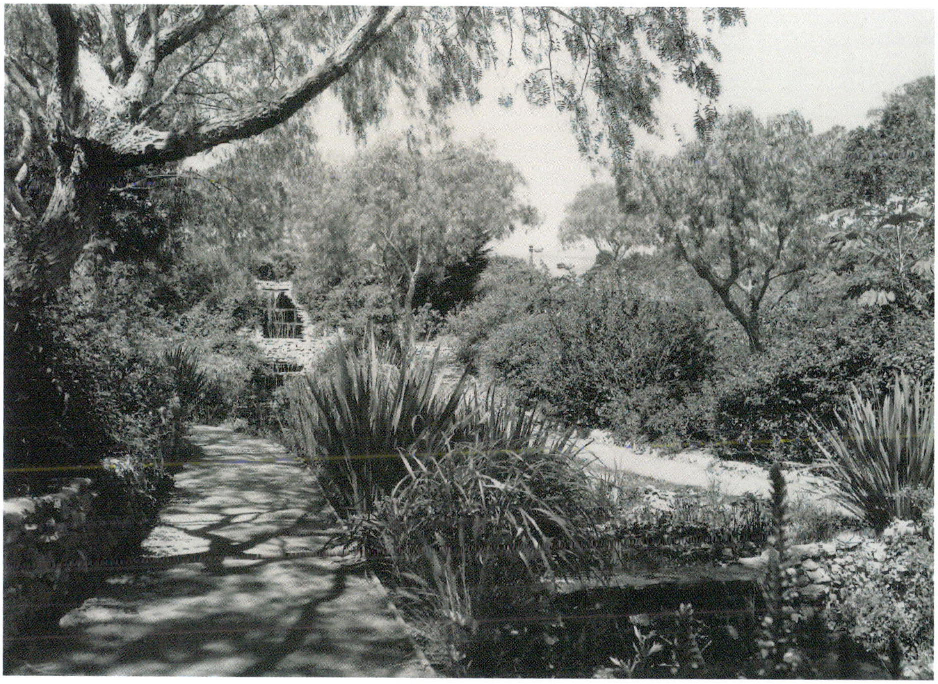

In 1922, a photographer made the above image of Averill Park's waterfall using a 4-by-5-inch view camera. This feature, which is located at the northwest corner of the park, is still enjoyed by park visitors today. Much of the foliage has been removed, and guardrails have been installed.

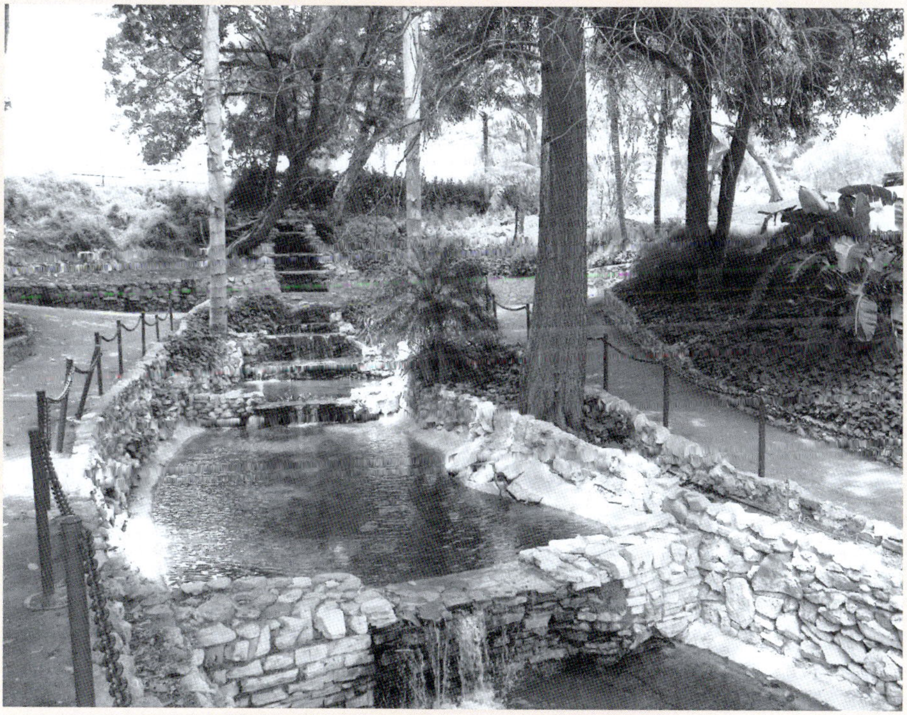

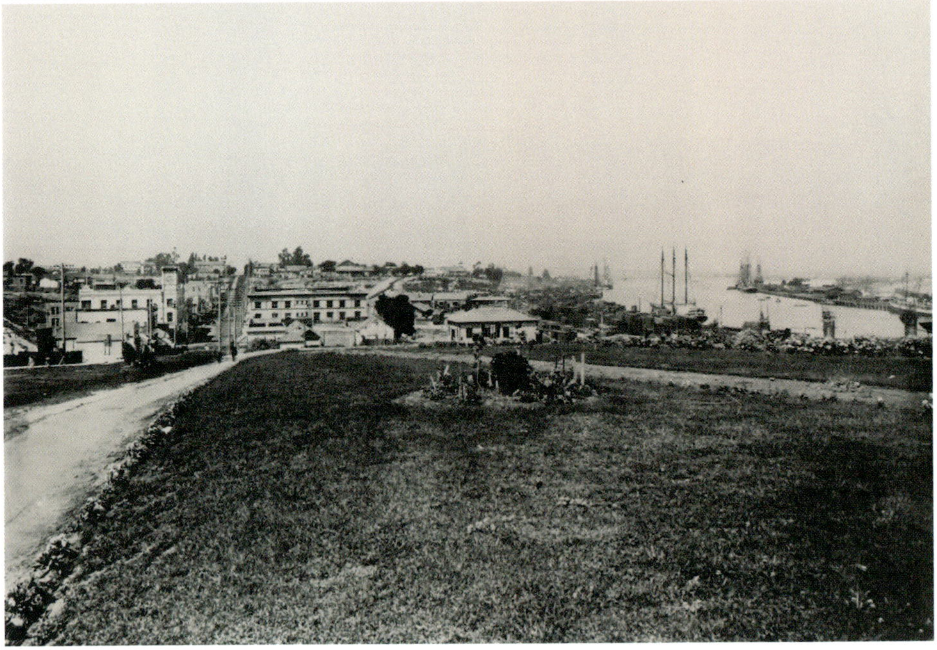

Taken in 1890, the photograph above is a general view looking north from what is now Ninth and Beacon Streets (Beacon Street is on the left side of the park). The clock tower of the Bank of San Pedro can be seen on the left just below the horizon. On the right is a clipper ship docked near the area where, about 50 years later, the municipal ferry building will be constructed. Close to where this photograph was taken, the Carnegie Library will be dedicated in 1906. Farther down the hill, San Pedro's second city hall will open around 1909, and the municipal building (pictured in the contemporary photograph) will open in 1928.

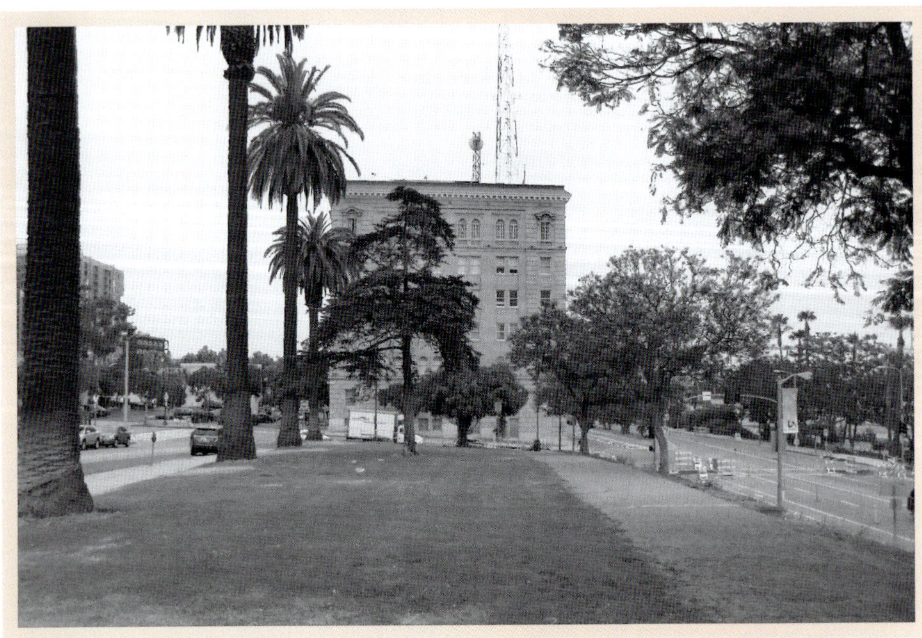

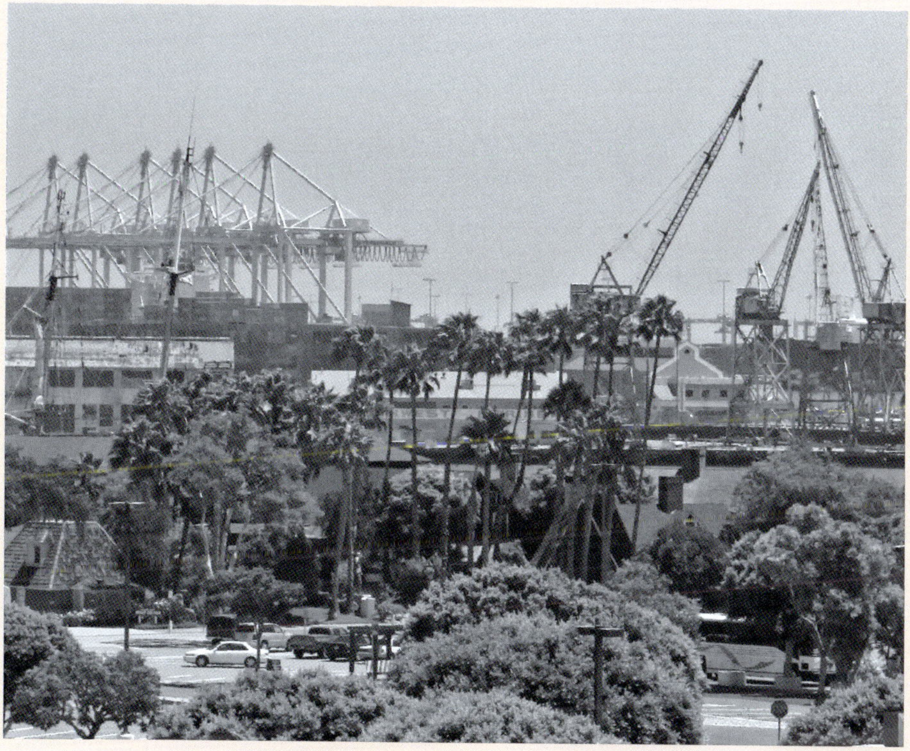

In the mid-1970s, a 375-foot "skytower" was erected in the parking lot of Ports O' Call. An elevator would take visitors up to a vantage point for a spectacular view of the Los Angeles and Long Beach harbors. After operating for about 10 years, an elevator motor broke down. It was never fixed or replaced. After a number of controversial business and political decisions, the skytower was sold to an amusement park in Detroit, Michigan, and dismantled in 1986. A parking lot now marks the site where the skytower once stood.

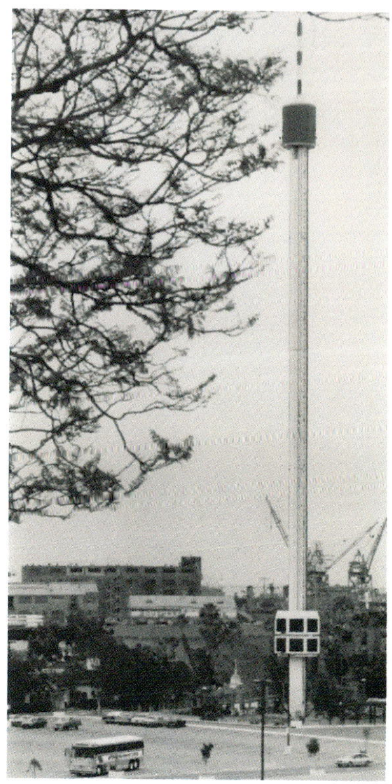